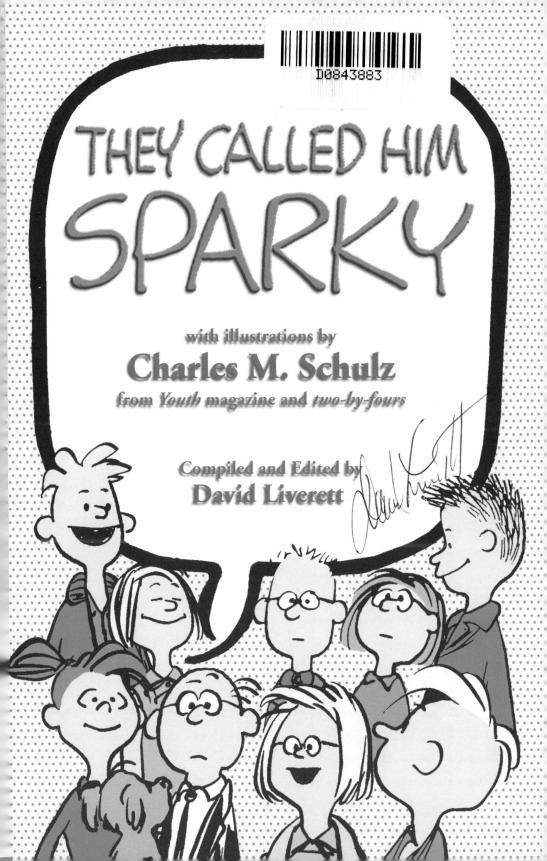

THEY CALLED HIM SPARKY

with illustrations by
Charles M. Schulz
from *Youth* magazine and *two-by-fours*

Compiled and Edited by
David Liverett

Chinaberry House
P. O. Box 505
Anderson, Indiana 46015-0505
www.2Lights.com

ISBN 0-9742410-9-1
Printed in the United States of America

Dedication

To my friend Harold L. Phillips (1913-2006), former editor in chief of Warner Press, who encouraged me in my art and publishing of books. While Harold was editor in chief, *Youth* magazine began publishing Charles Schulz's cartoons which became the source of three books: *Young Pillars* (1958), *"Teen-ager" Is Not a Disease* (1961), *What Was Bugging Ol' Pharaoh?* (1965). Also in 1965, the book *two-by-fours* was published with help from Kenneth Hall. The cartoons used in this book, *Remembering Sparky* came from the *Youth* magazine and *two-by-fours*. All of these cartoons were published while Harold L. Phillips was editor in chief (1951-1977) of Warner Press in Anderson, Indiana.

Foreword

Charles M. Schulz shared more than a wonderful world of cartoon personalities with people around the world. Sparky shared a deep gift of friendship ranging from some who knew an earnest young man in a tiny Minneapolis church to those who knew him across his years as America's premier cartoonist. They joined him in his constant search for truth, played golf or went bowling, listened to classical music, shared in service projects that benefited thousands of people.

Sparky's gift for friendship took him into a wide world of good and diverse friends, much broader than the little circle represented here. Most of those who have written here just happened to be in touch with him as a young man and early in his career as well as across the years. They are not any kind of elite inner circle. But they do offer interesting insights into the way his life was shaped. They found it good to know and love Sparky.

So come journey for a moment with these fortunate friends as they share in this book their rich memories of Sparky.

"I find the gospel very easy to understand.
What confuses me is theology!"

Table of Contents

Introduction

Much has been written about Charles Schulz, but in this little volume I hope to explore the early years of his life. As I contacted many of Schulz's friends in the St. Paul-Minneapolis area as well as in Anderson, Indiana, I was quickly reminded that those close to him affectionately called him "Sparky."

The first time that our local newspaper, *The Decatur Daily*, (Alabama) ran the *Peanuts* comic strip was Sunday, June 29, 1958. It pictured Linus having difficulty riding a rocking horse. He falls off but is comforted by his blanket. I don't have a memory of Charles Schulz or *Peanuts* until I attended the 22nd International Youth Fellowship Convention of the Church of God held in Houston, Texas, August 25 through the 28, 1960. I had completed the eleventh grade. Our youth group planned to make the trip from Alabama, but everyone was required to raise a hundred dollars to cover all individual expenses. A new chicken restaurant, Chicken Treat, had just opened that summer and they were looking for dishwashers. For the first time, I was drawing a salary that was recognized by the IRS. The money I made picking cotton in the fields of north Alabama in the 1950s was spent riding the Tilt-a-Whirl and the Ferris Wheel at the Morgan County Fair. However, the dishwashing money took me to the Lone Star State and to my first encounter with the art of Charles Schulz.

At the convention I was handed a booklet that had been illustrated by Charles Schulz. On the back of the booklet there is a cartoon character counting the medals on his sweater. The caption reads: "These medals are for Charles Schulz. All cartoons in this program are designed especially for the Church of God Youth Fellowship by Schulz, creator of *Peanuts* and *Young Pillars*."

After enrolling in Anderson College in 1964, I began attending Park Place Church of God and my Sunday school teachers were Kenneth and Arlene Hall. At this time, Ken and Charles Schulz were collaborating on the book, *two-by-fours,* with a subtitle, "a sort of serious book about small children," published in 1965 by Warner Press. The back of the book includes these words: "A small, unassuming book by Charles M. Schulz and Kenneth F. Hall about children in their second, third, and fourth years. Includes cartoons and text designed in an open-ended sort of way to help parents, grandparents, and other adults understand the small child, particularly as he relates to the church."

"I think I'm beginning to understand. . . . Going to church is something like having a night-light!"

The first telephone contact I had with Charles Schulz was in July 1969. My wife Avis and I made a trip out west. Before we left I called my former Sunday school teacher, Ken Hall, to see if he had Schulz's unlisted phone number. He gave it to me and as we approached Sebastopol, California, I called the number. To my delight Charles Schulz answered the phone. He wanted to meet with us and catch up on the news about his friends in Anderson, but he had a golfing date with his colleagues at United Feature Syndicate. Avis and I were planning to be in Los Angeles on July 4th and felt we couldn't stay until Schulz was available. He did give us his address just in case we could stay another day. The road that he lived on was Coffee Lane and the ranch was called "Coffee Grounds." Later that year the Schulz family moved about six miles away to Santa Rosa.

The man who created Charlie Brown, Linus, Lucy and Snoopy talks about Anderson College.

Advertisement for "Campus Life" October 1982.

By 1970, I was working for Anderson College designing all of their printed materials. Most of my work was with the admissions and recruiting departments. They had decided to ask Charles Schulz to recommend the college in a *Campus Life* advertisement. It was my responsibility to write to him with the request. After he agreed to send us a picture and a statement, I prepared the ad. This turned out to be one of my most embarrassing moments. I sent him a proof of the ad in full color. I made the mistake that several others had made in the past. He sent the proof back with a note saying that the ad looked good except "I don't spell my name 'Shultz.'"

The first time I met Charles and Jeannie Schulz was April 26, 1979, at the dedication of the Marvin L. Forbes Art Building which is part of the Ellnora Decker Krannert Fine Arts Center at Anderson College. Shirell Fox, Assistant to the President at Anderson College and my boss when I was employed there, had asked me to design the booklet for the dedication of the Fine Arts Center. After the ribbon-cutting ceremony, I was walking back to the car when Shirell called to me and introduced the two distinguished guests. There was such a crowd

Sparky signs autographs for Shirell Fox and students on the booklet designed for the dedication of the Fine Arts Center.

and I had thought I wouldn't have a chance to meet the Schulzes. I was honored to meet Charles and Jeannie. As an illustrator, it was a rare privilege to meet one of my heroes in the art world. I am one of the fortunate few who have taught classes in the Marvin L. Forbes Art Building. Anderson University is indeed blessed to have this first-class facility.

I had the vision for this book in the late 1990s and have been collecting writings from Schulz's friends over the years. My conversations with Jeannie Schulz have been very enjoyable. I appreciate so much her support of this work. I hope that by sharing some of the stories from those who have long loved the art and humor of this twentieth century philosopher, others will get new glimpses into the heart and soul of Charles Monroe Schulz.

Most of the stories and memories told by the writers in this book date back forty to fifty years. Some things reported as facts or as "the way things were" may be remembered differently by those who shared these experiences with Charles Schulz. Time has a way of casting a mist over details, and interpretation is in the pen of the writer. It is my hope that the reader will allow for any unintentional errors in facts and catch the spirit of the writers who consider themselves most fortunate to have known their friend "Sparky," and who love to tell their stories of him as they remember them.

David Liverett
May 4, 2006

Robert H. Reardon
President of Anderson College 1958-1983

Remembering Charles Schulz

I first met Charles Schulz almost fifty years ago in Anderson, Indiana. He had come to furnish the cartoons for a magazine called *Youth* edited by Kenneth Hall, a promising young author-editor of the Gospel Trumpet Company, the publishing arm of the Church of God. For several years, Sparky had been doing this without any charge. Kenneth and his wife Arlene had invited a small group of us to meet Schulz who was working out of an office in St. Paul, Minnesota. He was quiet and reserved, but came to life when we began asking him about his ambition to establish this infant enterprise with a major company like United Feature Syndicate. I was immediately drawn to him and was greatly pleased when I learned that they had indeed signed a contract with him in 1950. We became warm friends, stayed in touch, and this continued until he died in the year 2000.

When we met, I was the assistant to the president of Anderson College, and one of my responsibilities was to promote the school, particularly among the alumni. This brought me each year to the west coast for meetings in Los Angeles and San Francisco. The new Schulz home on Coffee Lane in Sebastopol was only a short distance from the Bay area and at his invitation I began to stop by each year. It was a joy and pleasure and our friendship grew. I slept in the old house which later burned and enjoyed the hospitality of Joyce and the growing family. Actually, the property developed considerably each succeeding year, Joyce being the developer and architect. It resembled a small, gated country club with provision for basketball, tennis, golf, and a soccer field. When I asked their oldest son, Monty, if he enjoyed all this he said that it was okay but that he really would prefer living in a regular neighborhood where you could just get on your bike and ride around to be with your friends. Kids have their own priorities.

Although Schulz was not a college graduate, I was quite unprepared when I walked into his library which was stocked with a rich collection of the great classics in religion, philosophy, history, and literature. I remember a good piano in the house and it gave me a chance to play parts of the Beethoven Sonatas I had memorized from my Oberlin days. Sparky was always interested in classical music and serious talk. We had many conversations about God, family, country, and the

"I received this set of Bible commentaries for my birthday. They're so beautiful I'm almost tempted to go into the ministry!"

world. His own spiritual pilgrimage began during his early days in the Church of God Sunday school and was nourished by the sermons, music, and the lives of friends. He studied the Bible and read and taught it with an open and curious mind. His spiritual formation grew out of a lifelong engagement with the teachings of Jesus, and what current religious scholars were writing. I still recall an interesting exchange we had on the subject,

13

"Does God need anything?" This of course raised the subject of public worship, particularly the praise music which he felt had begun to dominate contemporary church services. Does our God, the majestic creator and sustainer of the universe, look down and say "I'm not feeling so good today?" Things are not going well in my world. Come on give me a little more praise." It was his nature to think outside the theological box and he did raise the hard questions. But, I always found him to be involved in an honest spiritual journey with Jesus as mentor and guide. I am confident that the spirit of Christ was alive and at work in his life. It was this journey, I believe, that energized him to follow his passionate commitment to create.

"I'm glad you brought that verse up for discussion because I just happen to have a set of Bible commentaries with me!"

Early in 1972, I knew that there were some serious differences developing in his marriage to Joyce and on one visit I was aware of the strain and we talked about how painful it was. My training and experience as a pastor led me to suggest that it might be helpful to go to counseling. He let me know at once that he had considered and abandoned the idea. Their divorce soon followed.

By 1962, the comic strip *Peanuts* had captured the country and when I went to the Bay area I

approached Sparky about our interest at Anderson College in conferring on him an honorary doctor of laws degree. He seemed pleased but worried about days away from the drawing board. Few of us realize the enormous physical and creative energy necessary to prepare and mail in a fresh new script each week. Since he was afraid of flying it would be necessary to be gone for at least two weeks in order to make the trip to Anderson. But he was pleased and

Charles M. Schulz shaking hands with President Robert Reardon. Schulz received an honorary degree on June 17, 1963, from Anderson College.

agreed to make the trip. After agreeing to come, Sparky drove his Ford Thunderbird convertible cross-country to attend our commencement. I know the 7,500 of his fellow church members in attendance read his strip each day.

It was his first honorary degree and it may have been the first in the United States offered to a cartoonist by a college or university. At the time, elitist educational institutions did not consider the cartoonist a serious part of our cultural scene. However, time and Charles Schulz changed that, and the cartoonist's work began to be awarded the legitimacy it deserved. Countless recognitions

She and her husband had decided to attend a performance of King Lear.

It was their first night out together in months.

The manager of the theater walked onto the stage, and asked, "Is there a doctor in the house?"

Her husband stood up, and shouted, "I have an honorary degree from Anderson College!"

© 1974 United Feature Syndicate, Inc.

This Sunday morning "Peanuts" strip first appeared December 22, 1974.

followed with Schulz's characters on the cover of *Time* magazine. I have on my wall the *Peanuts* strip, which shows Snoopy typing a letter. The manager of a theater stops the show to ask, "Is there is a doctor in the house?"

As time went on I introduced my oldest daughter, Becky, who had recently come back from the Peace Corps, to Sparky. She was now making a living as a professional singer-entertainer at the Purple Onion in downtown San Francisco. It was not long before Sparky began using her in some of the films he was making, and in the yearly Christmas specials being filmed at the ice rink in Santa Rosa. In 1990, my wife Jerry went out to visit Becky who was working with Schulz on a television special called "Why, Charlie Brown, Why?" about a little girl with cancer. So, Becky invited her mom over to a recording session at Wally Heider's studio to sit in where the production was being made. All was going well until

During the second act one of the performers became ill.

It was at that moment when she decided not to get him anything for Christmas.

a problem developed. Sparky wanted Becky to sing "Farther Along" but the piano player didn't know it. Becky says, "We turned around and asked Mother if she knew the tune, and of course she did. We asked if she would be willing to play, and as usual she rose to the occasion and sat down at the big Steinway and recorded a beautiful piano track." When Sparky heard her play he said, "Now, that's what I wanted." The words written by J. R. Baxter spoke directly to the theme of the production and also to Sparky's own most profound theological questions.

After I became president of Anderson College in 1958, I continued to see Sparky when my responsibilities took me to California. By now, his readers were worldwide and in the millions. He had begun to move seriously into other media such as radio, print, films, and television, and I knew that he was being rewarded very well. Until this time I had never asked Sparky for any gifts for Anderson College, but I knew that sometime in the future there might be a project that would interest him. That time came in 1976.

I knew that Sparky had a special place in his heart for his former pastor, Rev. Marvin Forbes. Back in St. Paul when Sparky was trying hard to find some way to get his strip published, he was getting nothing but a large pile of rejection letters. The temptation was growing strong to give in to discouragement and the failure which continued to plague him. The dream was beginning to die. One Sunday afternoon, Pastor

Forbes knocked on his door and invited him to go for a drive. Forbes loved and believed in this young man, admired his talent, and did not want to see his dream die. So, in his gentle and quiet way the pastor assured him that God had a purpose for his life and that if he was patient, help from above would be on the way. "It was time," he said, *"to trust in the Lord with all your heart and lean not on your own understanding, to acknowledge Him in all your ways and He will direct your paths"* Proverbs 3:5-6. Then this humble and caring man asked God to fulfill his promise and give Sparky the strength and assurance needed. Not long afterward the Lord showed up and the *St. Paul Pioneer Press* and United Feature Syndicate signed a contract with Schulz. Sparky loved and honored his pastor for this encounter at a critical moment in his life.

"I see this is 'Spiritual Life Emphasis Week' in our church. . . . I wonder what it is that we emphasize the rest of the time?"

In 1978, Anderson College was at work in a major fine arts building construction project that would honor Ellnora Krannert, Wilbur and Eileen Schield, and Bill and Gloria Gaither. The structure would consist of four distinct units capped by an art gallery named for Jessie Wilson, wife of Charles E. Wilson of General Motors and later a member of President Eisenhower's cabinet. One of these buildings, I thought, ought to be named for Marvin Forbes and perhaps Sparky might be interested.

So I flew out to San Francisco and drove up to Santa Rosa to see Sparky in his ice rink complex office. I went with some apprehension because we needed one more major gift to complete the project. After greeting each other I confessed that I had come to relieve him of some of his hard-earned money. He picked up the phone and asked his business and financial manager to join us. When he came in, Sparky introduced me as president of Anderson College, and the chemistry in the room changed at once.

Before I could launch into my story, the young manager decided to get right to the point. "Fundraisers," he said, "were lined up at the door and that it was not an opportune time to be asked for any additional contributions." I was shocked and put off. So I turned to him and said that I had come two thousand miles to see my friend Sparky. I told him that it was my responsibility to explain to him what I thought to be an unusual opportunity to consider and did he understand that? Sometimes frank talk clears the air. I went on to say that if Mr. Schulz wanted to agree to my proposal, then it was his financial advisor's responsibility to tell him how best to do it. Sparky, who was amused, turned to me with a grin and said, "Okay, Bob, tell me what you have in mind." I felt better and went on at once to the project which would honor his former pastor and old friend, Marvin Forbes. When I finished, he asked a few questions, said he was very interested, and that it was something he would very much like to do.

On April 26, 1979, Sparky flew to Anderson to enjoy the dedication of the building. With his lovely wife Jeannie, he stayed with Jerry and me in Boyes House. At breakfast the four of us were joined by Rev. Marvin and Ruth Forbes. After coffee Sparky

Robert Reardon, Ruth and Marvin Forbes with Charles Schulz at the ribbon cutting ceremony for the dedication of the Marvin L. Forbes Art Building.

surprised both Jerry and Ruth with beautiful gifts, a Cartier solid gold Snoopy and chain for each as a memento of the occasion. The dedication ceremonies on April 27, 1979, were blessed with beautiful weather and a large and enthusiastic crowd. Since that time, thousands of students have attended classes in the Forbes building. They need to be reminded on occasion of a humble, interested, and loving pastor who spoke a word of encouragement to Schulz at a crucial time. It would also be helpful to consider what the world might have lost had he been silent.

Before he died, Sparky drove down Highway 101 to have dinner with Becky and me. By now, he was having some serious health problems and the conversation drifted to whether or not he might be retiring. "No way," he said. He intended to continue to the end and had made provision so that no one would take over further development of the characters he had created.

Sparky, like all of us, had a very tender spot and could be openly provoked when a writer or critic indicated that *Peanuts* was just simple "children's stuff." In 1965, Robert Short, a bright thirty-year-old seminary student from Dallas, wrote an engaging book titled *The Gospel According to Peanuts*. It turned out to be a national bestseller. In the book, Short takes the timeless concepts of the Christian faith and shows how these truths emerge through Charlie Brown and his friends. The human condition is all there in our strength and weakness, wisdom and folly, optimism and helplessness. The reader often sees himself in the *Peanuts* strip at the breakfast table in the morning. I once asked Sparky what he thought about the book and he said, "Right on." Short was right and the growing numbers of readers knew it. When Schulz died, he had 355 million of them in seventy-five countries. Incredible. It was one of the great pleasures of my life to know Charles Schulz.

In 2005, I was in Santa Rosa. Bob Coffman and I had a wonderful chance to be conducted by Jeannie through the new world-class museum she built so lovingly, to honor Sparky. Don't miss it, for it is an incredible collection of Schulz memorabilia and a dramatic presentation of his life and work.

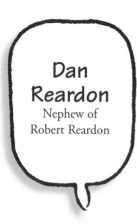

Dan
Reardon
Nephew of
Robert Reardon

Snoopy Drawing

On April 26, 1979, the Ellnora Decker Krannert Fine Arts Center was dedicated at Anderson College. Charles Schulz was there, as a benefactor and friend of the college.

Marvin and Ruth Forbes with Charles Schulz at Park Place Church of God the day of the Forbes Building dedication on April 26, 1979.

At a social function following the dedication, I saw Charles Schulz, a mere twenty feet or so away, and fortunately, I had in my hand a copy of the Fine Arts Center dedication program. I introduced myself, and asked Mr. Schulz if he would draw a "Snoopy" on the cover of my program. The hour was late, and he was obviously tired, but he graciously obliged. This was the first and only time that I had the privilege of meeting Charles Schulz. The Snoopy drawing, now framed, hangs next to a picture of our dog, Tucker, in our family den.

David Liverett, the artist who did the artwork for the cover and layout of the dedication program, is a longtime friend of mine. He has always admired the Snoopy drawing on the front of his artwork. David had talked with Charles Schulz the day of the dedication, but had passed up an opportunity for one artist to ask another for a Snoopy drawn on the cover of a dedication program.

Sometime around May of 1992, I asked David if he would draw a pen-and-ink sketch of my father from some photographs that I had taken earlier. David was happy to do that for me, and in jest offered to trade his services for the "Snoopy" that hung in our den, the Snoopy he always admired.

David's copy of the program for the dedication of the Fine Arts Center on which Schulz kindly drew "Snoopy."

David and I talked it over and I decided to ask Charles Schulz if he would draw a second "Snoopy" on a copy of the dedication program that David had kept. An explanation of our unusual request, with specific instructions as to where to draw the "Snoopy" on the cover, and a modest check for services rendered, was sent to One Snoopy Place, Santa Rosa, California.

The "Snoopy" came back in a week or so, perfectly centered between the artist's pencil markings, and the check was returned. What a gift Charles Schulz was to my generation, sharing the wit and everyday wisdom of his little people.

R. Eugene Sterner

Former minister and radio speaker

A Personal Tribute to Sparky

It was in Minnesota where I was guest speaker at a statewide Church of God Convention that I first met Charles Schulz. (Sterner remembers this date to be circa 1950.) He was a tall, slender, handsome man about ten years younger than I; he was introduced to me as Sparky Schulz. That was the name used by those who knew him and the name by which I have always known him.

Sparky was attending the congregation where Rev. Marvin Forbes was the pastor. Rev. Forbes had visited Sparky's mother who was dying of cancer and he had been so caring and compassionate that Sparky loved and respected him very highly. But Sparky was interested in the Church of God as a whole and wanted to know more about it. I was impressed with his sincerity and with his seeking mind.

He asked about our beliefs and what we stood for. I explained that we were non-creedal; that we were open to all truth and sincerely sought to learn all the truth we could; that we were open in fellowship with all Christian people and sought unity among all Christians; and sought to be led and used by the Holy Spirit. Sparky seemed to concur in those views. He wanted to know more about us as a fellowship and we talked about what the Church of God was doing; he wanted to know what we hoped for the future and I shared with him some of my own hopes and dreams. We parted as friends and I have been pleased to see his spiritual progress.

Some years later, several congregations in the Minneapolis-St. Paul area were planning a series of unity meetings and invited me to come for a week to work with them. I was delighted to be told that Sparky and his family had asked that I be entertained that week in their home. It was a precious time we had together. I have always remembered that time with gratitude.

Sparky was already being recognized as a fine cartoonist and as the years passed, this up-and-coming young cartoonist became more and more famous.

He showed me the studio that was provided for him by the local newspaper that carried his comic strip; he talked about how he got started in his work and about the frequent rejections and frustrations. But he persisted and thankfully, never gave up. It wasn't easy! I felt that I had been permitted to enter into his inner life and my appreciation for him increased. It was always fun to be with him.

My relationship with Sparky Schulz was never related to any business or in any professional capacity. It was simply a personal friendship as we shared about our own lives. Thus, my comments are about the man himself, his characteristics, his attitudes and his spirit. In my view he was indeed a first-class Christian gentleman, one of the most likable and courteous persons I have ever met. When I saw on national news the account of his colon cancer, then later of his death, I felt a deep sense of loss and grief. He was a brother to me and I loved him like a brother.

Sparky was genuine. He had the kind of integrity that came from knowing and accepting himself with both strengths and weaknesses. He was no phony; he wasn't trying to impress other people; he wasn't posing or pretending. He was realistic about himself. He was aware of his insecurities and idiosyncrasies and faced them honestly.

He had, also, that integrity that arises out of a clear purpose that was true to his own nature and his God-given gifts. He was a humble man who still had confidence in his own innate abilities. He had a sense of the will of God in his life, a sense of calling that would serve other people who were struggling within themselves. If anything comes through clearly in his comic strip *Peanuts* it is the presence of personal struggles, and he made them a blessing to countless thousands. His comic strip grew out of his own life.

Sparky was very congenial. He accepted other people as they were. He wasn't trying to make anybody over; he didn't argue about little differences. He was just himself and he allowed others to be themselves. I never heard him make a critical remark about anybody. He never made a disparaging remark in my hearing, but was always respectful and kind. He was warm and cordial with the quiet touch of understanding for those of us who have feelings of uncertainty. I had such feelings as many others do and I always felt better when I had been with him.

He had a gentle sense of humor. He seemed to chuckle about so many things, seeing the funny side first in himself, then in others. Sparky seldom told a joke, as a matter of fact he seemed to have some difficulty in doing so, although his humor was pervasive. He saw amusing things all the time. It was just part of his life. He told me, half jokingly, that

"Didn't anybody bring food?!"

his pastor, Marvin Forbes, was a real preacher. "He can explain the Scripture better than Dale Oldham or Gene Sterner." To myself I said, "Amen." His humor was unique and delightful.

Another characteristic of Sparky was his generosity. Our family was blessed especially when our oldest daughter was about to graduate from Anderson College. She was president of the Camarada Club and they were planning a special event before graduation. She asked me whether I thought we might persuade Sparky to come down from Minneapolis and speak to the club. It would indeed be special. I called him and he willingly agreed to come. The occasion was a huge success, the envy of many others who would have loved to have him. He was in our humble home for two nights. Our whole family loved him. Our daughter kept some of his drawings and cherishes them to this day. I wanted to pay his way but he jovially declined to accept even his expenses. We have never forgotten his kindness.

Later, after Sparky moved to Santa Rosa, California, I was on the West Coast for some engagements and having a little time to spare, I called him. He urged me to come for a visit. He showed me around the complex of buildings and his studio. As I was leaving, we stood side by side and he took my arm and said, "I'm glad you are my friend." I deeply felt his love. Then, being aware of my serious hearing impairment, he said, "Gene, go anywhere in the world where you can get help for your hearing and send me the bill." That's the kind of a man he was. My hearing specialist told me there was nothing that could be done and I told Sparky that. I have never forgotten his kindness.

When Anderson College was attempting to establish a fine arts center, Sparky contributed a substantial amount of the funding with the understanding that the art wing of the building would be named for Rev. Marvin Forbes. He wanted the honor for his early pastor. It was typical for him to remain in the background. He loved to give without recognition. That has been repeated many times in his philanthropy.

Many of us regard Sparky as a genius. His sense of the struggles of people and his sense of the eternal God is remarkable. This came through in private conversation and certainly in his little round-headed kids where so many of us have seen ourselves; in his subtle references to the Scripture and Christian living. With his subtle humor he has taught us about ourselves.

To draw and write *Peanuts* each day for fifty years had to be genius, and he did it all with his own hands plus numerous books and publications. He never would have claimed that he was a genius, but many of us thought he was. When the *Peanuts* golden anniversary book came out, he sent me an autographed copy and I cherish it fondly. When I read Rheta Grimsley Johnson's book *Good Grief*, I wrote Sparky a letter of appreciation. Then he called me and we had a little chat about old times.

Sparky Schulz has been acclaimed by countless thousands of fans. Some of the most respected columnists have praised him. Radio and television programs have featured interviews with him. With all my heart I pay tribute to Sparky Schulz. He is known all over the world but he was a dear friend to ordinary people like me. He was a gift from God to all of us. May he rest in peace.

"My Bible is holier than your Bible.
It has thinner pages!"

T. Franklin Miller

1910-2004

Christian educator and former president of Warner Press

Remembering Charles Schulz

I met Charles Schulz several times, but I could not say we were really close friends.

Largely through the influence of Harold Phillips and Kenneth Hall, "Sparky," as he was affectionately called, drew cartoons for three books and gave the royalties to the National Youth Fellowship of the Church of God, of which I was treasurer, and to Warner Press. *Young Pillars* was a set of cartoons prepared originally for *Youth* magazine, with Ken Hall as editor, and *two-by-fours* was given to Warner Press. As Executive Secretary of the Board of Christian Education, I corresponded briefly with Sparky on behalf of the Youth Fellowship and warmly thanked him for his gift of royalties and told him how the money would be used. As I recall, it was to help underwrite a youth workshop in Trinidad, West Indies. He was gracious but humble in his response.

Shortly after that, Harold Phillips and I were in Portland, Oregon, for the West Coast Minister's Meeting. We went down to the Bay Area of California and up to Santa Rosa, where Sparky lived. His house was a bit secluded but we found it. His office was in an adjacent building – more like a modest dwelling. He took us on a tour of his office – showed us works in progress, introduced us to his office manager and we talked freely.

He felt a loss that there was not a Church of God congregation nearby. He was attending a Methodist Church. He talked with enthusiasm about the Sunday school class he taught – young adults, mostly college age. He used writings from well-known, world-famed, authors on religion, philosophy, and social problems, as textbooks for the class. He was humble, sincere, well-read, biblically literate – almost a scholar.

We talked about the *Peanuts* gang and the personality of each one.

He had built a four or five hole golf course on his property so he could practice golf without going to a regular course. He hoped his children would take up golf. On his personal course one hole was long enough to use a driver, and I recall a short par three.

Sparky told me he had been invited to play a tournament at Pebble Beach. Maybe it was a celebrity tournament. Anyway, he was partnered with Tennessee Ernie Ford, the singer, with whom he found genuine Christian fellowship. I have seen Pebble Beach course, but never played it. There is one hole, maybe number eighteen, mostly over water – the Bay. When they came to the tee, his caddie handed him a number five iron, assuming he would not dare try over the water, but would take the safe "land" route – much longer and sure to call for an extra stroke or two. Schulz said, "Nothing doing! I have dreamed so often of standing here and driving this hole, hand me my driver." He went over, landing safely in the fairway and won the hole!

Sparky's former pastors: Marvin Forbes, Cliff and Jean Thor, Ruth and George Edes

He took us over to Santa Rosa to the ice skating rink he had built for the city so his children would have a place to skate. He took his family there frequently for family skating parties.

Sparky was a devoted Christian and dedicated churchman. He never forgot Marvin Forbes, pastor of the Minneapolis Church of God who frequented his father's barber shop. He had profound respect for Marvin Forbes and for Clifford Thor.

When I retired as president of Warner Press, Ken Hall arranged for Schulz to send an original cartoon of Lucy and Charlie Brown – emphasizing how fleeting and momentary is any noteworthy moment – such as a retirement party.

We chatted on a couple of other occasions, but not of consequence. He was a model Christian professional artist, a loving family man, an unabashed witness to Christ as his Lord and Savior.

Sparky's Pastor Remembers

As she looks back, Jean's most embarrassing moment in all of her life was when she asked Sparky, knowing that he was a cartoonist, "What do you really do?" At the time he was already becoming well-known in the field and the *Peanuts* cartoon strip was already popular. About six to eight months ago she wrote to him via email telling how embarrassed she was and still is about that question back in early 1953.

The Pastor's Class in the mid-1950s at the Minneapolis Church of God
(left to right): Bobbi Portinga, Jan Roshund, Pastor Clifford Thor, Vern Bjorndahl, and David Kriebel

Original drawing by Schulz for Jean Thor's baby shower.

We became acquainted in early 1953. I had just finished seminary. The First Church of God in Minneapolis was without a pastor. We were living in Minneapolis temporarily with my parents until a pastorate became available.

I was asked by the Minneapolis Church of God to fill in at the church. I did. Time went on. An older, active member of the church said to me in his Norwegian accent, "Why is it that you don't want to be our pastor?" At that time no one or no committee or board had approached me about being a candidate for the pastor of the church. After I was asked to consider pastoring the church, I served there until October of 1957. It was at the church we met the Schulz family, Sparky, Joyce, Meredith, Monte, and Craig. We never really got to know Jill and Amy.

If my memories are correct, the Minneapolis Church of God was started by the pastor and the congregation of the Merriam Park Church of God in St. Paul, where Sparky was attending. The Rev. Marvin Forbes was pastor at Merriam Park Church of God at that time. Pastor Forbes then became pastor of the new church in Minneapolis and I became the first full-time pastor of the First Church of God in Minneapolis. There were many wonderful people in this congregation including of course, Charles Schulz.

Memories of Sparky

Sparky's favorite pie was butterscotch. One day Jean made a butterscotch pie and he and I ate the whole thing in my office at the church.

It was known that his least favorite food was coconut.

One of the Schield brothers, who owned an earth moving machine company in Iowa, was giving the church a Hammond organ. Sparky and I drove to Iowa to bring it back.

"I think I've made one of the first steps toward unraveling the mysteries of the Old Testament. . . . I'm starting to read it!"

Sparky led a study on the entire Old Testament at the midweek services at the church. He was a very learned scholar of the Old Testament.

He attended one of the dinners we served at the parsonage for our Sunday school class. For several weeks we had a series of classes at the parsonage on "understanding ourselves" taught by a minister's wife. Sparky attended these sessions.

I had just finished seminary and money was tight for us. Sparky gave us a bond once a month for a period of time. Even though we were unable to let them mature, it was a help to us.

Sparky had very high regard for Pastor and Mrs. Forbes, for it was Pastor Forbes who ministered to Sparky's mother and father during the final illness and subsequent death of his mother.

We were privileged to speak to Sparky by phone, about two weeks prior to his death, a precious memory for us.

Little did we know in those years, our friend Sparky would become world-renowned and even following his death, new honors continue to be showered upon him.

Sparky followed in the footsteps of God and was a wonderful example of humility, love, and caring.

"As I stand here looking at the universe, somehow being recently appointed program chairman for the annual picnic no longer seems frightening!"

Madelyn
Hartman
Widow of
Marvin Hartman
and longtime friend
of Sparky's

Sparky Draws Marvin

Our meeting and becoming friends with Charles "Sparky" Schulz began in 1963 when we were invited to a reception following the awarding of an honorary degree to Sparky by Anderson College. We had heard about him before through good friends Cliff Thor and Ken Hall, and, of course, were readers of his strip *Peanuts*.

SCHULZ

"I hope my investing in a new set of tires doesn't give you the impression that I don't believe your preaching about the world coming to an end, Reverend Hartman."

There was an immediate rapport between my husband, Marv, and Sparky. They shared a common sense of humor, quick wit, and interest in the newest thinking in the field of theology. That friendship grew as Marv, on trips to the West Coast as president of the Board of Church Extension, visited Sparky in his office in Santa Rosa. I was with Marv on at least two of those visits. Sparky was always gracious and welcoming in spite of a heavy work load. The first question he would ask was, "Marv, what new books about theology are being written today?" Or, "What have you been reading lately?" After our chat, Sparky would take us to the skating rink he had built for the people of the town, and we would have lunch at a rink-side table.

I feel very privileged to have known Charles Schulz myself through those visits. He was never changed by success and all the publicity from the quiet, almost self-effacing man he really was. After my husband's sudden death from a blood clot in the main artery of his heart in 1986, Sparky never forgot me. He contacted me, expressing his own deep sense of loss, and I have spoken with him by telephone and sent him a book I felt he would appreciate.

When Sparky found out that our daughters were going to be married within three months of each other, he went to the vault and pulled out two original strips, which he insisted on always drawing himself. He signed their names and his, and they were thrilled. He also gave a strip to Marv and me, which has long been framed and cherished.

Two of our favorite things are a newspaper strip Sparky drew after hearing Marv had received an honorary degree from Anderson College. Marv was president of the Board of Church Extension of the

Church of God. The strip indicates the receiver of the degree as a "Dr. Hartman" and then proceeds to humorously spoof receivers of these degrees. Friends of ours from near and far mailed copies to us. One even framed it for Marv! My other favorite is a drawing of a young person looking at a clergyman and saying "I enjoyed your sermon on young people, Reverend Hartman....I almost got the impression that you were human once yourself!"

Since 1986, I have continued each Christmas, as have other friends of Sparky, to receive the special *Peanuts* calendar. I was especially glad to receive the 2000 calendar, as it is no doubt the last one.

"I enjoyed your sermon on young people, Reverend Hartman. . . . I almost got the impression that you were human once yourself!"

Another favorite I feel so fortunate to have is a colored drawing of Snoopy, laying serenely on top of a haystack, just contemplating. In the lower, right-hand corner Sparky wrote, "To my good friend, Marv." It is signed "Sparky."

I am so grateful to have spent a few hours of my life in the company of Charles Schulz and to have our family be the recipients of some of his creative, original art. Persons everywhere identified with his characters because he chose to be honest and take a chance, portraying them with all their foibles, weaknesses, vulnerability, and soul-searching problems. He himself admitted that he was Charlie Brown. In his characters we found ourselves, perhaps accounting for much of the success of the strip.

To many of us, Charles Schulz, you were a winner because you were humble in the face of great acclaim, always searching and open about your own feelings of inadequacy. May you, at last, have found total acceptance, unconditional love, and peace of mind, through God's grace. We miss you and found life richer and more fun because of your creative gifts in cartooning and just being yourself.

"We represent the young people of the church, and we've come to you because you're a minister and you know all about everything!"

Avis Kriebel

Longtime friend of Sparky's from his church youth group

The Little Church at 38th and 38th

In the 1950s we lived in Edina and Sparky and Joyce lived on Oliver Avenue. We had some church services in their home. Sparky was very active at First Church then. One Saturday morning, I as usual got busy making pies—Butterscotch— still warm from the oven, when to our surprise Sparky, Joyce, and the boys appeared at our door. Picnic style, we spread out on the living room floor to enjoy a piece of pie. Yikes! I had toasted coconut on the pie! [Coconut was Sparky's least favorite food.]

My daughter Sue had an invitation to Meredith's birthday party when they lived on West Minnehaha Parkway. Sparky had painted his trademark cartoons all around Meredith's room. The art work is still there according to a fairly recent news report. The car was so full of balloons for the party that the back wheels would hardly stay on the ground! It was after this that they moved to Oliver Avenue before moving to Sebastopol, California.

"Scholars have been disputing this passage of scripture for years, but this morning I'm going to give you the real scoop!"

41

I did lots of jobs at our little church in Minneapolis at 38th Street and 38th Avenue, as everyone had to do. I was the kindergarten teacher forever and so had Sparky's two boys, Craig and Monte in my class. I think Sparky and Joyce moved west before Jill and Amy were in my Sunday school class.

When my son David was in the service on his way to the Philippine Islands, he stopped at his cousin Anthony Kriebel's home in Palo Alto, California. Anthony took David up to Santa Rosa to see Sparky. Anthony had sold a pony to Sparky and they knew each other through "horse trading." Sparky had such kind and understanding counsel for David. We were touched. David was very proud to have received a "get well" card from Sparky after an appendectomy.

Under Sparky's leadership some of us read through the whole Bible. We had long assignments and were expected to keep up and complete them. I did and was proud to be able to do it.

A real fun night was the time that Paul Geske, Sparky, Bernetta Nelson, and I had a board committee meeting at our church. It was such a frosty, snowy, cold night. We scraped the windows and had only peepholes to see out. We were very creative and had such fun working together. We knew each other so well, had such fun working together—were pretty creative—and were such good friends. Our families grew up together.

I remember riding with Joyce in her pink Ford convertible to take our kids to our church camp, Camp JIM (Jesus In Me). David remembers riding with Sparky in his new black Ford to camp that year.

I once told Sparky that he should do a companion book to his *Teen-ager Is Not a Disease* and call it *Old Age Is Not a Disease*.

David and I visited Sparky in 1977. We flew into Sacramento and rented a car to visit relatives in Medford, Oregon. Before we boarded a plane for home we stopped unexpectedly at Sparky's studio. He put his feet up on the desk, leaned back and we talked—so typically. It was a bittersweet visit in many ways but Sparky was so warm and friendly, as always. He was a very special person to many, many people. Some of us are still receiving our annual *Peanuts* desk calendar! I think Jeannie must be cut from the same cloth.

I felt friends and acquaintances of Sparky's were coming out of the woodwork when he died, but undoubtedly we of the little Church of God at 38th and 38th were a unique and blessed group of friends.

First Church of God (1952) - Minneapolis, Minnesota

The church in Minneapolis first met in homes. One of these homes was that of Charles M. Schulz. He became acquainted with the Church of God when his mother was ill with cancer. Sparky was present when the pastor of the St. Paul Church visited her and served communion. He later testified of that service, "It was one of the richest memories I have."

Bernetta Nelson
Longtime friend of Sparky's from his church youth group

Bernetta Recalls Sparky

He was born on November 26, 1922, to Carl and Dena Schulz in Minneapolis, Minnesota. Two days later his uncle Monroe, also a barber like Carl Schulz, nicknamed Charles Monroe Schulz "Sparky" after Sparky the horse in the comic strip *Barney Google*.

Sparky, Wally Nelson, and Marvin Forbes.

Carl moved his family to an apartment in St. Paul and opened a barber shop there. Sparky attended school in St. Paul. His mother became ill with colon cancer. The family then moved to another apartment above a pharmacy and his barber shop. This move was made primarily because of Dena's severe pain and the pharmacist could just walk up the stairs and give her shots for the pain.

The Rev. George Edes of Merriam Park Church of God in St. Paul visited often with Carl Schulz in the barber shop where he always had his hair cut. Rev. Edes learned about Dena and thus the introduction to the Church of God. He faithfully ministered to her. On one occasion he had me come and sing for her. In 1943, Sparky was inducted into the army.

Two days later his mother died. Brother Edes had the service for her and Carl asked me to sing – my first meeting with Sparky. He asked that I sing accompanied by piano [because] "the organ would make the service too sad."

The Merriam Park Church of God choir directed by Faythe White, circa 1940.

Wally and Bernetta Nelson, 1942

Upon his return from the war he started attending Merriam Park Church of God – along with many returned veterans. And we all became great friends – spending our time in church, street meetings, playing hockey, tennis, and baseball.

I'm enclosing a picture of the pastors in the church who were very instrumental in Sparky's life. Brother Forbes and Sparky spent many hours together. Upon Brother Forbe's retirement, Sparky purchased a beautiful house for him. Cliff Thor was the pastor

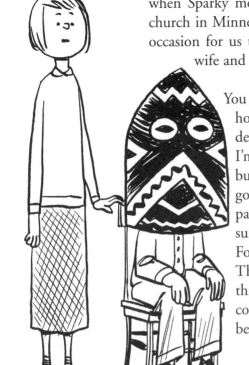

SCHULZ

when Sparky moved to California. By this time a church in Minneapolis had been built. It was a sad occasion for us to say good-bye to Sparky and his wife and five children.

You probably are aware that Sparky was honored in 1963 with an honorary degree from Anderson College. And I'm sure you know about the art building on campus dedicated to his good friend, Marvin Forbes, who passed away in 1989. Wally and I surprised Sparky, Marvin, and Ruth Forbes by attending the dedication. The pictures have deteriorated through the years. I attempted to have copies made, but they are not any better than the originals.

We have carried on our friendship via the phone and with letters for all these years. He never forgot us – his friends and the church.

I would guess that you have many clippings, but I'll include a few. Perhaps, you have copies of the biography, his fortieth anniversary book, and the Fiftieth Anniversary Golden Yearbook.

In the early days Minnesota didn't have many Church of God congregations – and we, in Minneapolis attended the Merriam Park Church of God. When Brother Edes was the pastor in St. Paul, a lot was purchased in Minneapolis to someday build a church there. When Brother Forbes was in the St. Paul church, it was decided that we should build on the lot. Until we had the building, we met in homes. Actually, three homes – Sparky's, ours, and one other.

Berny Berquist Falls

Widow of Maurice Berquist, a friend of Sparky's

Remembering a Call from Mr. Schulz

I hear you have been collecting some Schulz data! If you would get in touch with Gary Moore, who was Berk's associate in 1983, he will fill you in on Berk's association with Charles Schulz.

When Berk had his heart surgery in the fall of 1983, Mr. Schulz called and talked on the phone with Berk. He also sent flowers to the hospital. In 1992, Berk was seventy on August 8th. He received a delightful card – signed "Sparky and Jeannie." I still have it.

When Mr. Schulz became ill, I wrote and he had his secretary write and thank me. That was early in December 1999.

I hope all is well with you. I stay busy caring for terminally ill people. It gets a bit much, and I have to take a break now and then.

I'm looking forward to coming to camp meeting this year. Hope I see you sometime!

Sincerely,
Berny Berquist Falls

Gary Moore
Assistant to Maurice Berquist, former minister and longtime friend of Sparky's

"The Doctor Is In"

When we did the television special, "The Doctor Is In," Berk [Maurice Berquist] was the only direct contact with Schulz, and I was the only direct contact with Sparky's attorneys. It was my job to secure the legal permissions for the theme song,

"Sure, I can listen to the radio, watch TV, read a book, and talk on the telephone all at the same time, but I will admit that I'm glad breathing is automatic!"

cartoons, and personal appearances of Schulz. It was Berk's job to "sell" Schulz on the concept and his participation and to keep him interested in the project as it progressed. Berk and Sparky developed a good personal relationship during the project. Berk personally visited Sparky in California on more than one occasion.

Berk was a very creative person and I think that helped in his relationship with Schulz. They seemed to be in a world of their own. Schulz always took Berk's phone calls and seemed to thoroughly enjoy his conversations with him. Because of the relationship Berk was able to establish with Schulz, Schulz agreed to allow us to use any cartoon in print to illustrate the book Berk wrote for the special and to use cartoons in the special itself. He also agreed to appear personally in the special and to assign any royalties from the book or special over to us. The project took over a year to complete.

In addition to Sparky's printed humor, it was obvious that he had a quick wit and enjoyed matching wits with Berk. Berk would tell me about his conversations with Sparky. Many times the conversations ended with philosophizing and "solving the problems of the world."

It was obvious that Sparky was a very caring person and had a deep faith.

Helen Flynt
Longtime church
friend of
Sparky's from
St. Paul-Minneapolis

Remembering Sparky at Merriam Park Church

"I'm sorry, but I wasn't able to study the lesson for this Sunday. . . . The zipper on my Bible is stuck!"

Charles or Sparky as we called him, had just returned from overseas duty during World War II while I was still part of the youth group in the St. Paul Park Church of God (Merriam Park Church) and that's where I became acquainted with him. He became active in the church there and soon became a Christian. His father was the neighborhood barber that our pastor at that time patronized and it was through that connection that Sparky first learned of the church. One of his first published books of cartoons was one that he did for the Church of God, entitled *Young Pillars*. Most of the characters in the cartoons are named after those in our youth group. I was not as well acquainted with Schulz as some of the others in our youth group because I was married in 1946 and moved to Seattle about six months later. In 1952, St. Paul Park mothered a new congregation in Minneapolis and Charles Schulz became one of the leading laymen of that church.

Lee and Della Dibley were very close to Charles and his family. The two men served together on various committees. The Dibleys later became associated with the Bow Lake Church while we were there. About ten years ago I wrote to Sparky to ask him if

"Schroeder" in his comic strip had any connection with either me or my brother who was also in the youth group. He wrote a nice response to my letter, but said that "Schroeder" was named after a golf caddie that he had known at one time.

I'm glad that Ruth Forbes is still living so that you can get some good information from her about Sparky. Of course, I have always been a follower of the cartoons of Sparky because of his connection with the Church of God. His little book *Young Pillars*, which included so many characters from our youth group in the St. Paul Church so many years ago, is priceless.

Sparky certainly left a great heritage with his artistic talent coupled with his Christian perspective and outlook on life.

Frederick G. Shackleton

Sparky's pastor from 1944 to 1946 and longtime friend

Memories of Sparky

When I succeeded George Edes as pastor of the Merriam Park Church of God, St. Paul, Minnesota, in late 1943, I became acquainted with Carl Schulz, a member of the congregation, whose son Charles (Sparky) was serving in the U.S. Army.

Carl was George Edes' barber. When Edes learned that Carl's wife had cancer, he called on her. The Schulz family began attending the Church of God. Subsequently, Edes officiated at her funeral. This was just at the time Sparky was being inducted into the army.

I met Sparky in 1945 when he was on furlough. We became friends at once. We were the same age. When he returned to the military to complete his mustering out process, we exchanged letters several times. His letters frequently had drawings depicting activities we had shared, such as Ping-Pong.

"I have three jazz albums, two symphony albums, and sixty-eight religious albums. . . . If that isn't an indication of real spirituality, I don't know what is!"

When he was out of the service, we spent more time together, often including Doris, my wife. We played golf and exchanged home visits. He was a regular at church, although he had not yet received Christ as his Savior. We talked a lot about being a Christian.

"All right. . . . A motion has been made and seconded that even though Fred, here, interprets the story of Jonah and the fish allegorically, he can still be permitted to attend our Youth Fellowship picnic. . . ."

One time in my office I was urging him to commit his life to Christ. We knelt together in prayer. But then he said, "I'm not ready for this," and we got up. He didn't make that commitment until Marvin Forbes followed me in that pastorate. Later, he wrote to thank me for my part in leading him to Christ.

In June 1946, I left St. Paul to teach at Anderson College. We kept in touch. When our son, Martin, was born in December 1947, Sparky expressed as much excitement as one can in a letter. Eighteen months later we visited in the Schulz apartment over the barber shop and Sparky's dad gave Martin his first barber haircut.

In 1949 or 1950, Sparky wanted to meet with the editor of the *Gospel Trumpet* and asked if he could stay with us. It was an enjoyable visit. This was the visit mentioned in the book *Good Grief*, by Rheta Grimsley Johnson, on page 134. "His memories of Church of God Bible studies and camp meeting in Anderson, Indiana, are vivid, some stained with the increasing customary bouts of depression: 'I remember taking the train down once. I stayed with good friends and was having a wonderful time. Then, on the third day I felt terribly lonely.'" In a thank you letter he drew himself lying on the floor with Martin sitting on his stomach saying, "Hi, Sparky."

After Sparky became a Christian he was very active in the youth group. He put an ad in the St. Paul newspaper, at his own expense, presenting key doctrines of the Church of God as stated mainly by Charles E. Brown. (This has no connection to the *Peanuts* character.) He became an avid reader of Church of God literature.

In 1957, I think it was, we visited Sparky at his ranch, the *Coffee Grounds*, near Sebastopol. When we got out of the car and I was admiring the beautiful grounds, he made a wide sweeping gesture with his arm and said "Behold the power of the American comic strip!" We stayed a couple of days. Sparky and his wife, Joyce, had five children and we had three. The children hit it off well. Sparky and I played golf and tennis and talked nonstop.

When they moved to Sebastopol they had visited the nearest Church of God. It was a small and struggling congregation. They chose to attend the local Methodist church. Sparky spoke well of the pastor.

Sparky taught the adult Bible class for several years. He told me that when he accepted the assignment he immediately ordered Church of God materials from Anderson and used them in the class. Later he taught just by going through the Bible.

On a subsequent visit I learned that he was no longer teaching. He said, "We went through the Bible two times and after that I didn't have anything more to say."

We visited him again in Santa Rosa after he married Jeannie. Things were going much better for him now. The children were grown.

In a recent telephone conversation he said that he thought the teachings of the Church of God were right but that not enough had come of it. That is a statement it is easy to concur with.

Sparky did not identify with the Church of God in the West. I don't know of any Church of God people in California other than ourselves who were in his circle of friends. I think he had not attended any church regularly for many years. In the book *Good Grief,* on page 137, he is quoted as saying, "I do not go to church anymore, because I could not be an active part of things.

It is true that early on Sparky had a clear identity with the Church of God, first in St. Paul and then in Minneapolis. He did not maintain that relationship in California. He did make a significant gift to build the fine arts center at Anderson College but on the condition that it be named for Pastor Forbes and not for himself. He had a retirement home built for Marvin and Ruth Forbes when they retired. All this points back to a loyalty to his Minneapolis friends.

"Our discussion group misses you, Fred. When you're not there, we don't have anyone to leap on as soon as he opens his mouth!"

Photo taken in 1949

Letters from Sparky

January 4, 1949

Dear Fred, Doris, and Martin Lynn,

There is no doubt in my mind that you, Fred Shackleton, next to me, of course, are one of the most remarkable men roaming the earth today. I saw the song you wrote for the convention, and heard the chorus that was sung on last Sunday's radio program. Sensational! I also heard *My God and I* not long ago. Sensational! I have also heard your recent solos. Sensational! That's a real program, and I get an enormous thrill out of listening to it.

How is my friend Martin Lynn? Have you taught him how to hit those long tee shots yet? Or have you taught him how to play Ping-Pong? No, of course not. How foolish of me. To teach one, one should be able to play better than the pupil.

Heh, heh, heh, heh, heh.........Riotous laughter!

Seriously, the radio program is truly inspiring. We broadcast over station KBTR here. This is strictly an FM station, so some people in the congregation do not feel we are doing much good. Of course we could never afford a bigger station, so I am of the opinion that we should go along as best we can. We

have pledges of a dollar a week to keep us on the air. This is not easy. We are short on pledges, and sooner or later are going to be way behind. So far we are just holding our own. I just want you to know this in case you folks doing the actual program ever get discouraged that people are hearing you, and are appreciating what you are doing, please remember that we appreciate so much we are having a rough time keeping going. (That was an odd sentence, but I think you know what I mean.)

I have a brand new huge radio-phonograph combination now with the long-playing attachment. This is really something. An entire symphony on one record! I have been buying symphonies and concertos like mad. My latest purchase and favorite is Beethoven's second. A long cry from Hazel Scott, eh, Doris?

Second Page

Page two? This was the second sheet wasn't it? Well, yes. Then it must be page two. What are you trying to do?

I have been thinking of doing a little song writing myself. What do you think of this for a melody?

Ta ta te ta ta da da te da da da da te te ta ta

"I nominate Fred for program chairman because he's a young man with ideas and lots of drive and because we all know that nobody else will take the job!"

This is just a thought more or less. You realize that. I am figuring on using this little melody in the Scherzo of my symphony number one. I figure on opening the first movement with a cymbal solo. This will last for approximately fourteen bars. I am leaving it more or less to the discretion of the conductor. Various conditions will govern its length. Weather, ticket sales, etc. Then eight men come in from the wings carrying bass fiddles over their shoulders, and at the same time breaking into the main theme which will closely resemble *Go See What the Boys in the Backroom Will Have*. This not only concludes the first movement, but it also concludes the bass players' contracts with the orchestra. The second movement is sort of sad. Some will say that I am morning for a lost loved one. Mourning that is. The truth will be far from it, however. These melancholy passages were picked up one day at work when a lady was heard humming a weird bit of music.

"That's lovely," I said to her. "I didn't know you could sing."

"Sing, nothing," she answered. "I've got my foot caught in the desk drawer!

The third movement as I said will be the scherzo. Now for the climax. At the beginning of the fourth movement the entire orchestra will stand, while the conductor remains seated. This gives quite a striking effect. The music itself in this movement is monumental. By this we mean it sounds like someone pounding on concrete with a sledge hammer. All the French horns play *La Marseille* while the violins break out with some splendid little passages closely similar to the sound made by closing street car gates. I have already had this symphony recorded on a new type of cardboard record I have invented. Absolutely no surface noise. In fact no noise whatsoever!

I sincerely hope that you are all doing well. Someday if you can manage to find time, I wish you would make a record for me. I'm sort of partial to *There Is a Fountain*.

I wish I could write long newsy letters, but they just aren't my style. I am sorry I didn't get down to see you last summer. I would really have liked to, and most certainly would have if it could have been done. I still plan on doing it. I promise you.

You two were instrumental in leading me to Christ, and I appreciate it. This makes us permanent friends, and I know I am getting the best part of the deal.

As, ever,

Sparky

June 29, 1949

Written after the 1949 Anderson Camp Meeting

Dear Fred and Doris,

I am writing this with the sincere hope that Martin still is waking up, and starting each day by saying, "Hi, Sparky," eight times. I miss that. I also miss the bacon and egg breakfasts by the open window.

The trip back was completely uneventful, which is just the way I like my trips. I sat several seats behind Doctor Linn [Otto F. Linn], and didn't get to talk to him at all, for I didn't wish to interrupt anything he and Mr. Gray [A. F. Gray] might be talking about, although I would have liked nothing better than to have spoken with him a while.

It was a real treat for me to meet and see some of these people whose spiritual books I have studied. There is no doubt in my mind that the Church of God is it. So firmly convinced am I of this that I have been instrumental in having this series of articles run in the St. Paul paper weekly. I believe that I mentioned them to you. I thought you might care to see what they're like, so am enclosing one. Naturally any suggestions will be taken gratefully. Also I do not pretend to be the author of any of these. I have merely taken portions from the writings of Brown, Riggle, Smith, Mary Baker Eddy (whoops) (skip that last one) etc. Note that we are stressing and tying in the same slogan as is used on the radio.

It seems sort of strange to get back to my rattly old '34 Ford after cruising around in that huge yacht of yours. I think instead of putting on the brakes when you park, you should merely throw out an anchor!

What a car. It was so wide I had to take a taxi to get from one door to the other. The headlights were so far apart it looked like the lights they have on each end of Montgomery Ward during the holiday season. I think you almost need a copilot. I was always afraid of falling against one side, for you see, I bruise like a grape! Be careful of those fangs, Lassie!

This photo of Sparky and Fred Shackleton in front of his Redwood Empire Ice Arena was taken circa 1975.

At church tonight the choir was getting ready to rehearse your latest song. Dolores was also imparting to them some of the things you taught in your class. I don't know any more of what went on, for I then left.

I hope I was able to put over to you my appreciation for your putting up with me under such trying circumstances. Poor Doris, trying to get all the meals straight with people coming and going right and left. What a remarkable young lady.

I just bought Beethoven's sixth, so now have all of them but the third.

We've got to get in another golf game if you come up this summer, and I most certainly do hope that you do. It is something that I have come to look forward to each summer, and I also know that the congregation gets a real blessing when you sit up front, and sing as in days of old. I've two sets of clubs, you know, so if your car is packed, you can save yourself that bit of taken-up space.

I'm sorry that it has taken me this long to write, but you know how hard it is to get everything done. I suppose I should be dropping Harold a line as soon as possible too. Good old Harold.

By the way, I'm thinking of writing a couple [of] epic poems. See what you think of the titles. *"He grabbed her by the collar because he liked to hear her holler." "He grabbed her by the gullet, as he shot her with a bullet."*

Maybe I should stick to my writing of symphonies.

Don't let us down this summer. If you're in this area, please stop in.

As ever,

Fred Shackleton's Letter to Sparky

June 3, 1989

Charles Schulz
Santa Rosa, CA

Dear Sparky:

When Cindy Drews learned that I knew you, she wrote the enclosed letter to you and asked me to send it. I wanted to write an explanatory note about her.

Cindy has shown great courage and determination to achieve in spite of being "disadvantaged." She was born with the enlarged head syndrome and survived with difficulty. As her writing shows, she has some neural problems. But she is in college because she is indomitable. And she is making it, though she is not a quick learner. With her own physical problems, she is especially sympathetic with others who have difficulties.

If you can respond to her, it would be wonderfully meaning full to her.

Doris and I remember with nostalgia and affection the "good ole days" when we were in your company more often. I hope we will have that privilege again.

God be with you!

As ever,
Fred Shackleton

Sparky's Letter to Fred Shackleton

June 15, 1989

Dear Fred:

Thank you for sending along the letter from Cindy. We have answered her and hope it brings some pleasure.

Obviously, I think about Doris and you very often, and it is always with good memories. Unfortunately, we have lost many of our good friends since those days and, of course, I speak especially of Harold Ramsperger.

Brother Forbes and Ruth have not had much success with their retirement because of many health problems, but are still struggling along. The Minneapolis church seems to be doing well and progressing in its care for people.

"Here comes Harold. . . . The first time he says, 'Let's greet the brethren with a holy kiss,' he gets slugged!"

As ever,

Sparky

Dora and
Loren Nelson
Longtime church
friends of
Sparky's from
St. Paul-Minneapolis

"A Great Inspiration to All of Us"

In the late 1940s, I was in the same youth group with Charles (Sparky) Schulz at the Merriam Park Church of God in St. Paul, Minnesota. We all knew him as "Sparky." He was very devoted to the Church of God and was an active member of our youth group.

I will never forget one evening Sparky was in charge of the games at one of our youth meetings. Since he was an ardent artist even then, he chose to have us all draw various animals. He handed out our assignments to draw. Since I can hardly draw a straight line with a ruler, I thought, "He will never miss the animal he assigned to me." To my chagrin he did notice and I was required to draw an elephant, doubtful that even he could recognize what it was. We did have a lot of fun in our meetings.

The youth came out in force to attend the New Year's Eve event at the church. After the meeting at church we all piled into cars and went to Minneapolis to an outdoor skating rink. We sometimes played hockey. One particular New Year's Eve the skating rink was not frozen enough to skate on, so we went to one of the homes in Minneapolis and waited for the rink to freeze enough for us to skate. After several hours we all gave up and went to our respective homes.

Rev. Marvin Forbes and his wife Ruth pastored the Merriam Park Church of God in St. Paul when

Sparky attended there. They were both active in the work of the church. Sparky was very attached to the Forbes.

Sparky lived with his dad over his dad's barber shop on Snelling Avenue in St. Paul, Minnesota.

"Other people put a shell to their ear and hear the ocean roar. . . .He hears Handel's Hallelujah Chorus!"

Sparky corresponded with me while I was attending Pacific Bible College in Portland, Oregon. He studied his Bible regularly and thought perhaps he would enroll at Pacific Bible College, but he never did enroll. I think a young lady caught his fancy and he married her.

He wanted to draw cartoons for our church publishing company youth paper. But the church was not ready for cartoons in the youth paper. He was ahead of his time and it wasn't until later that Warner Press accepted his cartoons for publishing.

Sparky was a great inspiration to all of us who knew him. In his cartoons he could express things in a way people accepted.

Sparky, we do miss your cartoons but the contribution you have made to our world will be long remembered. Rest in peace!

Ruth Forbes

Widow of
Marvin Forbes,
Sparky's pastor from
1946 to 1953
and longtime friend

Memories of Sparky

Charles M. Schulz in his early twenties was home from military service (WW II) in France. His mother had died while he was still in active service. His father, a barber, spent most of his time at his place of work. Sparky (everyone called him that) was an only child, so I was told, who was lonely and sad at times. One probably would not guess this because of his sense of humor and much chuckling.

Ruth & Marvin Forbes,
Sparky & Jeannie Schulz

It was soon after we came to St. Paul that Sparky walked by the church one morning, saw the new pastor filling in the bulletin board out in front of the St. Paul Church of God. He walked over and introduced himself. The pastor, Marvin Forbes, invited him into the church building for it was very cold outside. There they became even more acquainted.

From that day until the new church in Minneapolis was finished, Sparky was always faithful in attendance, helping in any way he could. Sparky was a part of the group that established a new church in Minneapolis.

We left there and took a church in Indiana [Goshen], and Sparky stayed during Cliff Thor's ministry and 'til he (Sparky) moved from Minnesota. While in St. Paul, Sparky attended art school, then taught art, but he still found time to visit the pastor often.

"I wish ol' King Herod had been here, Brother Forbes. . . . You would have had him all shook up!"

Several times a week Sparky came to our house. Our whole family welcomed him and we had many happy hours talking mostly about the Bible, church doctrine, books by church writers such as: F. G. Smith, H. M. Riggle, and Charles E. Brown. Sparky was eager to learn **all** he could about the Bible and the Church. There was root beer—a bottle for each one. Years later, Sparky referred to the times when we drank root beer as we discussed the Bible and the Church of God.

The phone rang about 2:00 AM one morning. It was Sparky. He was very excited. "I'm convinced. I see it, I see it! My conclusion is: the Church of God is it! No doubt about it." As far as I know, he never lost that vision of the Church of God, nor his conviction that the doctrine of the Church of God was absolutely correct.

A few weeks before Sparky's death, I had asked him about his church life and his beliefs. This was something we mentioned now and then throughout the fifty years I knew him. His answer to the question I had asked him was, with a chuckle, "I haven't changed anything, I still believe the same as always."

Of all the times we were together in person or talked on the phone or read his many letters, Sparky was the same humble Christian, generous, fair, honest, a friendly gentleman. It seemed he never changed. His riches, fame, nor the fact that he was a celebrity did not turn his head one way or the other.

I would say Sparky fought a good fight; he kept the faith and is now at home with the Lord.

All of the memories of Sparky are good ones.

"Brother Forbes' preaching on Sodom and Gomorrah never fails to thrill me!"

Ruth Forbes
Widow of
Marvin Forbes,
Sparky's pastor and
longtime friend

As I Remember Sparky

Sparky's first car was a one-seat sportster. One day Sparky came to our home which was four rooms attached to the side of the church. He was downcast and unsure of the future of his comic strip career. Brother Forbes and Sparky walked to the Mississippi River which wasn't too far away. They found a place on the bank of the river [and sat] for a long while as they dealt with the issue. When Sparky was ready to go into the Sunday morning colored comics,

"I think the presence of my car does a lot for our church. . . . It proves we're a struggling young congregation!"

his instructor suggested he change the name perhaps to *Peanuts*. Sparky wasn't too fond of the idea. He liked the name he had chosen, *Li'l Folks*. Right away, I liked the name and told him so. We all hashed this over for a while. Somewhere along the way, Sparky agreed to call his comics *Peanuts* which stuck for fifty years. Sparky moved to Colorado Springs, Colorado, for a short stay and came back to Minneapolis and eventually bought a ranch in northern California.

Ruth Forbes
Widow of
Marvin Forbes,
Sparky's pastor and
longtime friend

A Gold Necklace
and a Home

Charles Schulz and his wife, Dr. Reardon and his wife, my husband, Marvin Forbes, and I were all dressed and ready to walk across the street to the Anderson College campus to begin the day-long celebration of the dedication of the Fine Arts Center on the campus. Sparky reached into his pocket and pulled out two small red boxes. He opened the boxes one at a time, put one gold necklace around Mrs. Reardon's neck and one around mine. He snapped them securely, then it was time to go. We both wore the Snoopy necklaces all day.

Robert Reardon, Ruth & Marvin Forbes, Sparky & Jeannie Schulz cutting the ribbon at Anderson College's new Fine Arts Center. Schulz dedicated the Forbes Art Building to Rev. Marvin Forbes.

Sparky, Ruth & Marvin Forbes, at Anderson College's new Fine Arts Center.

So many memories I have of Sparky over the last fifty years, all good ones. Now last but not least. How can I ever forget? We tried to plan for retirement because Pastor Forbes was by now beginning a long bout with Parkinson's Disease. Sparky and Pastor had talked about our retirement. Then Sparky discussed it with me to see what we would like. I told him we would like just a small house with a yard all around the house so we might have a few flowers and maybe a small vegetable garden. He had thought of an apartment, condo, townhouse, or whatever. When I mentioned a house, Sparky replied, "Then a house it will be!"

We have been able to finish our last years in a real nice house in a real nice neighborhood. Brother Forbes did enjoy making a garden for the first four years. I am eighty-five now and still live here. Not a day goes by that I haven't felt grateful for our home and many times thanking Sparky for his love, friendship, and generosity.

Letters from Sparky

November 29, 1955

The Forbes were pastoring in Nowata, Oklahoma.

Dear Brother Forbes,
We all saw your article in the *Gospel Trumpet*, and were very proud and excited. Apparently your writing course has done much to help you already. I know that you'd want to know if Wally Nelson, Wally Ortman, Bus and a few others had seen it, so I thought I'd better write immediately.

Everything around here is about the same. We are talking of expanding the church here because of growing Sunday School problems. Seventy-five per Sunday is beginning to be the average figure.

Please greet Ruth and the kids. We miss her and them very much, and of course, we miss you, too. I hope to see many more such articles.

As ever, Sparky

January 10, 1956

Dear Ruth,
Thanks very much for sending me the clipping from *Youth*. I was pleased that you had seen it, and were able to make some use of it in your church. The cartoons will be appearing every two weeks from now on, I guess.

We have just finished a week's joint revival meeting here with the St. Paul Church. We had Rev.

R. Eugene Sterner from Anderson as evangelist.

The Wally Nelsons and us were talking last fall about driving out to see you some long weekend. Maybe we can accomplish it this next year, although Joyce's expecting another baby might put a stop to such a trip.

Anyway, we wish you the very best of everything. You people are living examples of what people should be like, and we miss you very much.

Sincerely,
Sparky

June 1, 1956

Dear Marvin and Ruth,
I doubt very much if it would be practical for us to make a trip out there this summer, for Joyce would not be up to it. We are expecting the baby early in August, and she could never never ride that far comfortably. However, it would be SWELL if you would drop in on us. We have plenty of room both in our house and in our hearts for you, and would be very happy if we knew for sure that we could look forward to seeing all of you. O.K.?

As ever, Sparky

September 7, 1956

Dear Brother Forbes,
I really appreciated your taking time out from a busy schedule to write me such a long letter. It certainly was wonderful seeing you and Ruth and Bonnie and

Patricia again, and everyone to whom I have spoken remarks on how well you all look.

You need have no fear that we shall do anything to attempt to undermine the Mpls. work here just to get you back. As you have said before, the Church of God is bigger than any one person, and I shall have to see God's leaning before doing anything. We are at a complete stalemate anyway, and I do not have the slightest idea as to what the future of our church is or even what the majority of the people want. I believe always in cooperating with whoever is pastor, and trying to follow his ideas.

It would be nice of course to have two churches in the city, but I could not even say what the opinion of the people is on that. I am a believer in riding the waves until the doors of direction open up. Now, if you were to take the St. Paul Church, we would rejoice even with having you that close again, and would come to see you often, but in case it has been a point of wonder with you, I doubt if the Mpls. people would drift over there again. Most of the church pillars here believe in working in their own storehouse. I say that in case you fear that your returning to St. Paul would draw from Mpls. and your modesty would prevent your expressing the thought yourself.

Once again may I say that it was a real thrill just to talk with you again. Someday, I hope you may be able to return to our midst, and if the chance comes for my working toward that end, I most certainly shall.

Yours in Christ,
Sparky

November 13, 1956

Dear Marvin,

I am surprised that you have heard nothing from the St. Paul congregation, for I know for certain that Bro. [George W.] Buck has taken a church in a suburb of Wichita, Kansas. Perhaps you shall get word from them yet. I don't know what is going on over there, for I haven't had a talk with any of them in some time.

Everything here remains the same. Of course with Ike back in, business is booming and the area is confident of prosperity and peace. (Two Thunderbirds in every garage.

[unsigned]

October 3, 1957

Dear Bro. Forbes,

The main reason for my not answering all of your letters is that I just have nothing new to add to all that has been said and done in this business so far.

I can certainly understand your feeling that maybe you should change your mind, and withdraw your name from our list, but please do not feel that there is any real element against you. I honestly have not heard of any such thing. The reason for asking for references from you was only to make certain that the whole procedure was done properly, and that no one could say that the many people who want you to come back pushed your name through. We on the pulpit committee agree with you that these references are mostly a mockery, for we really do not expect to get any bad ones on any applicant. In fact, being on this committee has convinced me that the whole business of pastoral selection is a slipshod one at best. No wonder there are so many mistakes made.

I am going to be gone for almost this whole month now so I did want to write you a few lines before we left. I have to go to Oregon to speak, and from there to Chicago to autograph books, and from there to Anderson, Indiana to attend a new Business Men's Organization that is being formed by the Church of God. What I am really trying to do is become head of the whole movement so I can have things my own way.

Please greet Ruth and your family, and remember, whatever comes of all this, we still hold each of you in the highest regard.

Sincerely, Sparky

October 23, 1957

Dear Brother Forbes,
I just wanted to drop you a note to let you know how glad we are that you will be coming next week.

Could you write and tell me when you will be getting here? We are inviting you and Ruth to stay with us. Also do you plan to have extra meetings, or preach only on Sunday? We certainly would be glad to announce extra meetings if you wish to hold them.

Regards.
Sincerely,
Sparky

No Date

I am sending you a copy of my new book so you won't have to go out to buy one. You would do well to study it carefully, for it contains great theological truths that are hidden beneath the surface, and lie there to be discovered only by the scholar who is willing to devote his life to diligent study.

Kindest regards, and please greet the whole family,
Sparky

August 28, [1963]

The year was not indicated but the letter reference to "sitting up on that platform that night knowing you were in the audience" may refer to his receiving an honorary degree from Anderson College on June 17, 1963.

Dear Ruth and Marvin,
We haven't treated you very fairly not letting you know all that happened after we left Anderson. For that I apologize. Being with you both those two days meant more to us than we can ever tell you, and the memory of our praying together in the motel room will always be with me.

Craig was very glad to see us when we got home, and his spirits rose after their being quite low. The doctor said it was the worst break he had ever seen. He was in traction for a month and then after we brought him home, he had to be in a cast up to his waist for five weeks. That cast is now off, and he is under the daily care of a physical therapist who is helping him to regain his walking. He has been very good through the whole thing, and has complained almost none.

Marian [Marian and Bus Reid were an aunt and uncle to Sparky.] died about three weeks ago after lingering far beyond the time given her. It was a very difficult experience for Bus, but he has come through it all quite well. He is continuing to live here with us, and this helps him for otherwise it could be lonesome. Our kids like him a lot so it is good for us too to have him around.

I hope everything is well with you folks. It meant a lot to me sitting up on that platform that night knowing you were in the audience. (Even if Marvin did almost fall asleep!) I hope we shall be able to get together again sometime soon.

As ever,
Sparky

September 29, 1966

Dear Marvin,
Sometimes it takes me a long time to answer letters, and sometimes I never get them answered at all, but I did want you to know that I appreciated your thoughts and words concerning my Dad.

He had only been here a day and a half. He awoke early Sunday morning, about 4:00 A.M., with a chest pain. Of course, this sort of thing had been going on almost nightly, but this time he sat up to take a pill, evidently couldn't find one immediately, and fell back into bed. He probably died within three or four minutes although we worked amateurishly on him for half an hour waiting for the ambulance to come. Our one consolation was that he at least had completed his mission, which was to get here to see his grandchildren.

Harold Ramsperger and his family spent several days with us this summer, so we had chance to talk over old times and new theology. Now there's a title for a sermon, "Old Times and New Theology." Makes your mind whirl with ideas, doesn't it?

Our best to Ruth. We miss you both.

Your friend,
Sparky

P.S. I am certain that many were blessed by your most recent article in *Vital Christianity*.

September 14, 1973

Rev. & Mrs. M. L. Forbes
2020 Andrew Street
Fort Wayne, Indiana 46808

Dear Ruth and Marvin:
Lots of things have been happening to me, and although I am not a good letter writer, I hope to be able to let you in on at least, the main news.

I plan to remarry in about a week to a very kind woman who lives here in Santa Rosa. She is a gentle little girl, and I know you would like her very much. I was greatly tempted to ask Marvin to come out to perform the ceremony, but I didn't want to obligate him.

We have purchased a very nice home overlooking the city, and would have room to accommodate you easily, if you are ever in California and can find time to stop by. I know we could spend the whole night talking and I hope that it will happen.

I have been back to Minnesota only once in the last fifteen years, and that was to make a speech in Moorhead at Concordia College where my oldest son, Monte, is attending. I saw Richard and Georgine Geske at that time and it was as if no time had passed at all. We laughed and talked and reminisced and thoroughly enjoyed ourselves.

My best to both of you.
Love,
Sparky

"I've come to see your daughter, Mr. Ramsperger. . . . I'm one of those awful teen-agers you read about in the papers."

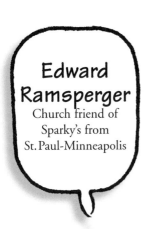

Edward Ramsperger
Church friend of Sparky's from St. Paul-Minneapolis

Sparky As My Best Man

This is just a few notes to tell you about Sparky. This is a picture of our (mine and Norma's) wedding, May 1, 1949. Sparky was my best man. Sparky was our Sunday school teacher at the Church of God, 330 North Pryor, St. Paul, Minnesota. The class was called *20/30s*. Our class was small but we all loved the Lord. We had some beautiful times. The years were 1948, 1949, and part of 1950. We had some very good times playing ice hockey. Sparky moved to West Minnesota and got married. Later he moved to Sebastopol, California, and I lost trace of him after his move. But had a good memory of him as my close friend.

Norma Jean and Edward Ramsperger's wedding, May 1, 1949.
Left to right: Evelyn Kippels Ramsperger, Ruth (last name unidentified),
Norma Jean Ramsperger, Edward Ramsperger, Sparky, and Kenneth Nelson.

85

Shelli Ramsperger Spriggs, Elaine Ramsperger, "Sparky" Schulz and Mary Ramsperger Peterson, May 1997 in Santa Rosa, California.

"Would our church's future missionary to New Guinea kindly tell me what he was doing down at the drugstore with Elaine Ramsperger instead of me?"

Elaine Ramsperger
Longtime friend of Sparky's from his church youth group

In a conversation with Elaine Ramsperger, she related to me that her husband, Harold, was probably Sparky's best friend. Harold died in 1972 at the age of fifty-two. Harold and Sparky loved the cartoon character "Krazy Kat" and also great music. Elaine and Harold's son sent a copy of this much treasured drawing that captured Sparky and Harold's diversity in the arts. Elaine's daughter, Shelli, and Sparky's daughter, Meredith, are about the same age. Shelli remembers falling asleep in Sparky's studio while her dad and Sparky listened to Bach and Chopin.

Original drawing by Sparky.

"Five dear friends gather for an evening of music"

She told me that the only time Sparky was the worship leader was the time that former pastor, Fred Shackleton, came back to Minneapolis for a concert. Elaine sent me a recording of the service. Sparky loved teaching his young adult Sunday school class and on many occasions had "chalk talks" during the church service.

David Liverett

Charles M. Schulz

Letters from Sparky to Kenneth Hall

January 28, 1957

Dear Ken,

Thank you very much for letting me know of the reaction to the *Youth* cartoons of the lady from Ohio. Things like that are always encouraging.

I was glad to hear that you had seen the article in the *Post*, and can assure you that it was not 75% accurate, but 100%. That's the way it goes.

Kindest regards, Sparky

October 29, 1958

Dear Ken,

I really am quite pleased with *Young Pillars*. You did a perfect job on the inside layout, and the cover actually isn't too bad. I appreciated your sending me the ten copies.

It was good also to hear that we will be doing so much good with the royalties. For once I think my meager talent may be doing some work for the Kingdom of God. Every now and then I think back to the days when I would have been very happy to have accepted some sort of job with the Gospel Trumpet Company. I think it would be the greatest thing in the world to be able to associate daily with men like yourself, Brother Sterner, Brother Reardon

"Don't cry so loud. . . . We're trying to sing, 'Our Church Is Such a Happy Place.'"

etc., but I guess we must labor in different fields.

I was asked recently to contribute my reasons for believing in immortality for an article that is to run in *Better Homes and Gardens*, and when I wrote only a few words, and quoted mostly from Jesus, the man who is in the position of gathering together these articles wrote to tell me that my article was too short, and he had taken the liberty to add a few sentences. In these he used the example of a dying fire and a quotation from Longfellow to back up what was to have been my views so I had to write to tell him either to run it my way or forget the whole thing. Don't I have problems?

Regards.
Sincerely, Sparky

March 16, 1959

Dear Kenny,

Thank you for letting me know about the situation with *Gospel Light*. It was for this very reason that I originally asked you to be the chief policy-maker because I certainly have no information about any of these people, and their relations with our movement or others with similar ideas to our own. This is the way I work with United Features, and this is the way I hope we can continue to work with the youth cartoons.

Because there is no Church of God in Sebastopol, I have been attending a Methodist Sunday School. Am I excommunicated?

Regards, Sparky

October 6 [1963]

To the Editor,

"We were singing, 'Jesus Loves Me' when all of a sudden it hit me. . . . Jesus loves me . . . ME . . . completely worthless ol' me!"

The fears that Chief Justice Achor and others who have written in our weekly magazine concerning Supreme Court rulings against school prayers show a profound lack of faith. The success of our Lord's teaching and the survival of the early church was due to its holiness. It needed no government approval. If our spiritual lives need the support of governmental laws, then we are already doomed. The basic teaching of the Book of Revelations is the triumph of God's true church in spite of all that goes on around it. Our faith must lie in the ability of the Gospel to save the individual. The Gospel does not need the law on its side. "If God be with us, who can be against us?"

Sincerely,
Charles M. Schulz

July 21, 1964

Mr. Kenneth Hall
Gospel Trumpet Company
Anderson, Indiana

Dear Kenny,

I received a phone call from the *Chicago Tribune* this morning. They are going to start running "Young Pillars" which they like very much. Thought you would like to know.

Regards, Sparky

May 21, 1965

Kenny Hall
Gospel Trumpet Company
Anderson, Indiana

Dear Kenny,

The number one reason I haven't been sending cartoons for the past few deadlines is that I've been trying to cut back on all my extra activities until I began to feel better.

If I try to write too many cartoons and write too many books it results in my stomach hurting, and nobody loves a cartoonist whose stomach hurts.

Your friend, Sparky

July 8

Dear Kenny,

Here are the two latest cartoons, one of them appropriate for the Booksellers daily newspaper, I hope. The more I think about the project, the book about the nursery child, the more I am inclined to think I won't be able to do it. At least this does not seem to be the kind that could be done with only cartoons. It is going to need explanatory text with maybe cartoons to accompany it. How does this sound?

"They're starting to pray again. . . . This is where we came in."

Our two days in Anderson were a treat for us. Joyce was especially taken with you and your wife. I wish we lived closer. Sometimes I think God purposely denies me this "land of promise" of close Christian companionship. Talking with you and Alan [Egly] and Brother [Marvin] Forbes and George Buck, etc. does wonders for me, but maybe I am meant to dwell alone behind a drawing board.

I hope something works out with Determined Productions. At any rate I think we can turn out an even better Youth cartoon book this time. Again I thank you for your hospitality and thoughtfulness.

As ever, Sparky

May 8 [1965]

Sent when submitting finished art for two-by-fours

Dear Kenny,

Here you are. The little blue marks at top and bottom are for your layout man. They will help him to keep each cartoon straight. Will I get to see the book before it goes to print? I would like to check it through first to make certain that each drawing is right. Hope you like them.

Best regards, Sparky

Hall and Schulz, Rogers and Hart, Gilbert and Sullivan, Landon and Knox

August 26

Dear Kenny,

I wrote to the lady who didn't like the cartoon. Thanks for sending me the information.

The article from *Decision* has brought quite a response. Lots of letters from all over. I suppose this sort of thing does some good especially to encourage young people. I have received several letters from such readers saying so, but I will never get over the feelings of guilt over being lauded publicly when so many others who appear to be "least in the Kingdom" are really the "greatest in the Kingdom." This is why I shy away from having you reprint the article. However, if you think it will do any good, then you may, but please know that I tremble with fear for being built up too much. People don't need me, they need to "see Jesus only." I know you understand, and I trust your judgment.

As ever, Sparky

No Date

Schulz sent this letter from Sebastopol to Ken Hall in the style of a telegram.

Dear Kenny,

Absence of *Youth* cartoons due to extra heavy schedule STOP Everyone and his mother wants cartoons STOP No longer have time to draw comic strip STOP Man here from Hallmark for three days STOP Am going quietly crazy, but no one knows it STOP Forgive me STOP Will try to get back on schedule this week STOP. Professional pride at always being able to meet deadlines seriously damaged STOP

Best regards, Sparky

"Whatever happened to the good ol' peaceful Sunday morning breakfast?"

Kenneth Hall

Collaborated with Sparky on the book "two-by-fours" and served for many years as an editor for Warner Press

Memories of Sparky

"I'm proud to say that I am not the least bit jealous of my baby sister. . . . Isn't that perfect proof of a humble spirit?"

By 1953 *Peanuts*, launched through United Feature Syndicate in 1950, was a hot cartoon, growing rapidly after a slow start and becoming the "in" thing with cartoon lovers across the country. I did not see it regularly because the *Chicago Tribune* had a regional franchise on it, and it did not appear in Indianapolis or Anderson. But I knew that its creator, Charles M. Schulz, was a Church of God layman in Minneapolis. At about this time his new pastor, Clifford Thor, talked with me about getting Sparky involved in doing some things for the church.

Cliff and I had been in school together at Anderson College in 1944-45. At this time I was youth editor at Warner Press, and it occurred to Cliff and me that it would be great to have Sparky do a regular cartoon for the weekly *Youth* magazine. So, I called Sparky and got a favorable reply. He would clear the project with the syndicate, and away we would go. But United Feature Syndicate said no. They didn't want their young cartoonist draining away his creativity or diluting his market with this "side" project. He was also doing a weekly sports cartoon feature for Sunday papers in addition to *Peanuts*.

We kept in touch. A year or so later, after his fame and standing had grown still further, he told me that he thought things would now work out. "This time I'm not going to ask them. I'm going to tell them." I have always been surprised by his determination to do this project and by the way he carried it out, meeting every deadline with his meticulous and thoughtful work.

We started running the single panel cartoons we called *Young Pillars* every other week in *Youth*. My boss, Harold Phillips, was initially very concerned about what the reaction would be. But the humor was so gentle and generally pastors and other church leaders were so proud to have this man cartooning for the church that the response was overwhelmingly enthusiastic, positive, and supportive. Sparky himself thought we were pioneering with this sort of material in a church publication, and expressed that feeling much later in his biography, where a chapter gave a lot of attention to this phase of his life. Actually church publications had been carrying cartoons ahead of this. David C. Cook even had a Bible cartoon book kind of publication in *Sunday PIX*, which was much criticized by many educators and Bible scholars. The depth of insight into human nature and the general quality of Sparky's cartoon series was unprecedented in the church field.

Other church publications were quick to notice *Young Pillars* and wanted to reproduce it. So with Sparky's permission we got into the syndication process. We charged a small fee to cover costs and, at Schulz's request, turned this income over to a writer training program we set up at Warner Press.

In May, 1958, the annual meeting of editors of church magazines for children and youth was to be held in Minneapolis. Since Sparky was living right there, the program committee noted, wouldn't it be good to get him to speak for our conference? And at the same time a number of editors wanted me to interview him for a personality profile article that would be syndicated in our field. So I brought this all up with Sparky during our regular contacts in the months ahead of the May conference. In the process of doing the cartoons, we had developed a habit of contacting each other frequently, often not about business.

"Just when I was getting strong enough to be able to defend myself, they start telling me about sharing!"

I received many notes of just one or two sentences, often a postcard addressed to "Good ol' Kenny Hall." I found later, after his office had to start screening tons of mail for him, that I could be sure to get my note through if the envelope was addressed to "Good ol' Sparky Schulz." We enjoyed a repartee of give-and-take with each other. Our humor did not involve telling funny stories, just a sharing of human observations that seemed funny to us.

Sparky agreed to speak to the editors' conference, which was to be held at a downtown hotel. We planned to meet for lunch a day in advance. At that time we would talk about the article I had been asked to do on him. By that time a number of popular magazines had carried biographical pieces on him, one of the best being in *Psychology Today.*

We met for the first time in the hotel lobby, I recognizing him from the pictures I had seen in magazines.

He was tall, slender, three or four years older than I, with a ready smile and laugh lines around his eyes. We hit it off immediately, but he didn't want me to do the article. He didn't think he was a good enough model to be written up in church magazines. There was that persistent humility, even shyness. He thought a church magazine was always risking something if it wrote up people before they died. But at length, after quite a bit of fun over how good a model we each were, he decided to let me give it a try. The next day he wowed the editors as he recounted the development of the principal characters in *Peanuts* and drew sketches of them. Later I wrote the article, and it was published in perhaps fifty church magazines across the next year or so.

By coincidence, Sparky was going to Anderson for the weekend just at the close of the Minneapolis conference. He had agreed to speak for the spring formal of the Camarada Club at Anderson College, an event he had agreed to participate in through his friendship with R. Eugene Sterner, whose daughter was a Camarada member. Since Sparky was averse to air travel, we arranged to take the train from Minneapolis down to Anderson. We visited, discussed the Church of God, talked theology and philosophy, much of the way down. Finally, just as we bumped and rattled our way into the Anderson station on the old Pennsylvania line, I heard Sparky muttering to himself as we wrestled with our luggage: "Sparky Schulz, what are you doing in Anderson, Indiana, anyway?"

He did well in Anderson, entertaining at the formal and then on Sunday night doing his illustrated lecture on the *Peanuts* gang in the sanctuary of old Park Place Church to a near capacity crowd that had come in for an expanded session of the College Youth Fellowship, for which Arlene and I were advisers. When I went to the Sterner home to pick him up for the Sunday evening schedule, he was out and running a little late. Bob Reardon had latched onto him and had taken him on a tour of the Anderson College campus. When Sparky came in, he told me, "I think I'll leave my money to a home for old cats." Fortunately for Anderson College, he did later contribute generously to the school, and he also accepted an honorary degree in 1963.

"My name is Walter. . . . I'm three years old, and I've come to get religion!"

Another event of 1958 was the collecting of the first group of youth cartoons into a Warner Press book entitled *Young Pillars*. Once again there was some concern on the part of management about how well this would do and what criticism it might draw from the conservative book market Warner Press was serving. It sold "like hotcakes" and drew universal high praise. Sparky had indicated that the royalties should go to the Church of God Youth Fellowship at the National Board of Christian Education. It was the first of three books in this series, compiled from the cartoons that originated biweekly in *Youth*.

It should be noted that at this point *Peanuts* itself was about to reach a crescendo of popularity across the nation and around the world. The whole enterprise had not yet reached very far into the licensing field where it has flourished in most recent years, but the cartoon series itself was receiving unprecedented adulation. There had never been anything like it. No television specials had yet been developed. No Broadway play. No books carrying theological analysis. A couple of books reproducing the cartoons themselves. No endorsements of MetLife or Ford. Yet by 1959 and 1960 the cartoon was on every tongue, being cited from about every pulpit. And its creator was being known as an earnest churchman who didn't drink or smoke and whose work was squeaky clean.

It was at about this time that the Schulzes decided to move west. Sparky told me that he would have been content to live in Minnesota the rest of his life, but that Joyce was restless. He felt burdened for the small church in Minneapolis in which most of his closest friends worshiped. His own financial support was by now greater than all the rest of the church's income, his pastor said. Sparky himself realized that was not a healthy thing for the church. At the same time Joyce was uncomfortable with the church connection and seemed to resent the responsibilities he was carrying in it. On the other hand, California beckoned. He agreed that he would like better weather for year-round golf and outdoor tennis. The winter sports he enjoyed around Minneapolis would be within reach from many places in California. Soon the family was established outside Sebastopol, not far from the coast, just up from San Francisco.

In the 1960s an interdenominational committee was working on a new vacation church school curriculum. As a part of that they wanted to produce a small book that would help to educate parents and workers with preschool children about the nature of these children and how the church expected to work with them. Mildred Hatch, the Church of God representative on the committee, came to me to see if I would write the book and get Sparky to illustrate it with cartoons. I was interested, and so was Sparky. So we started talking and writing back and forth about the project. Eventually it was decided that I would go out to California and spend some time putting the project together. We made

"One more songbook, and I think I'll almost be able to see the preacher. . . ."

an outline in advance. He would sandwich into his regular daily routine some time to meet with me and go over what I was writing, and he would sketch some illustrative cartoons in the process.

So Arlene and I flew out to San Francisco, rented a Ford (the *Peanuts* gang had just started appearing in Ford commercials), and drove up to Sebastopol, north of the city, where the Schulzes were then living on "the Coffee Grounds." We made our way past some grazing sheep and playing children, and found Sparky in his studio. We lived during our week or so visit in the guest house, which was attached to Sparky's studio. He was immersed, of course, in

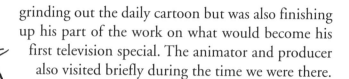

grinding out the daily cartoon but was also finishing up his part of the work on what would become his first television special. The animator and producer also visited briefly during the time we were there.

We soon met Sparky's wife Joyce, who was at the time an architectural student, and the five children up at the main house. The place was furnished simply with much activity centered around a huge family table. The walls of the house were already lined with fine art, most of it, as I recall, contemporary.

"God loves me. . . .
God loves me not. . . .
God loves me. . . .
God loves me not. . . ."

The daily routine began for Arlene and me with fixing our own simple breakfast in a kitchenette attached to our living quarters. Then I would meet with Sparky at his drawing board, and we would discuss the chapter we would be working on that day. All the time his pencil would be flipping about sketching this or that. After about a half hour I would go off to his excellent library where there was a typewriter, and would go to work on text for the chapter. Sparky would be dealing with his mail and other matters with the young woman who was his secretary and general assistant and at the time his only employee. About midmorning we would get back together for a coffee break and update on how things were going, particularly on my end of things. He would also show me what he had cooking on the day's project of drawing *Peanuts*. After the morning's work was completed, we would get together for lunch, usually sandwiches fixed there or something Joyce brought in from a fast food place. By midafternoon we would get together to pool our thoughts and work for the day. A given day would usually yield one nearly complete cartoon sketch and four or five typed pages, rough draft, for the book we began to call *two-by-fours*. With much of the day's work behind us, we would often have extended chats at this time. Here are some of the areas of conversation that I now remember, if only vaguely, from this and other visits during the 1960s and 1970s:

- The San Francisco pro teams, especially the Giants. We talked sports quite a bit. But Sparky was more interested in participating in sports than in talking about them. He had played golf from high school on. He was a good tennis player. His interest in ice skating and hockey was backed by his construction of the ice rink at Santa Rosa where he skated almost every day.

- Public school education. He was critical of it at that time. Would anybody in the Church of God be interested in establishing private Christian day school education in northern California?

- Concern about the safety of his children. The Schulzes were just coming into big money, and there had been a lot of publicity about the two million dollar contract he had just signed with Metropolitan Life. He was afraid of kidnappings. He was afraid of being hit with huge suits over even little accidents he and Joyce might have while driving.

- The Church of God. He was committed to its ideals in unity and church membership. He was not particularly impressed by its "denominational" development. He liked simplicity in church organization and worship.

- He felt embarrassed by his lack of formal education, but you could also see his confidence in what he had learned along the way and how he was keeping up with things. He had an excellent library, especially for biblical studies. He received a flood of the most significant current magazines.

- He shared observations, often humorous, of church people we both knew. He recalled the days when he taught a tiny class of hard-of-hearing old folks in the Minneapolis Church. One of his class members was an elderly man who rode his motorcycle everywhere, including from Minneapolis to Anderson Camp Meeting. Another time he rode that cycle down to Independence, Missouri, to see Harry Truman. Sparky was very loyal to old friends.
- One of the people Sparky most admired was Marvin Forbes, his pastor during some crucial years. Later Sparky would have a wing of the Krannert Fine Arts Center at Anderson College named in honor of Marvin rather than for himself.
- He shared his more recent experiences of teaching. At this time he was teaching an adult class in a nearby Methodist Church. (He would continue a study of the Psalms across a two-year span.) He loved Bible study and knew how to do it on an in-depth level.
- It was hard for him to picture a God with all the trappings of an Oriental potentate. It was hard for him to visualize a God who would demand to be worshiped and praised. We may want to do that out of our own hearts but not out of any divine command. This was a theme he returned to with me several times across the years, including a visit with Don Courtney and Ken Prunty years later.
- His love for dogs was evident in our conversation and in the way he dealt with pets around the *Coffee Grounds*. He understood their self-absorption, just as that was revealed in Snoopy. His dislike of cats showed up, just as it would be reflected in references to the cat named World War III in the strip. He joked about the "low intelligence" of the sheep on the *Coffee Grounds* but still loved the critters.

- He talked about his work habits. He wanted to do every stroke of *Peanuts* himself. He wasn't interested in getting ideas for the strip "sold" to him by others. He wanted to make sure that the strip ended with him, just as the work of any author would end with that person. He wanted to maintain tight control of any spin-off products, any licensing arrangements. He was tremendously concerned with the quality of these spin-offs.

- He regarded himself as more of a writer than an artist; perhaps better, more of an author than an illustrator. He felt that the main part of his work was in creating the story line that developed the personality of the characters involved. He was not particularly interested in creating sight gags, although he would occasionally do that. He felt that by keeping his drawing very simple, the focus could be more on the ideas.

"Hi! I've just been told that I'm one of God's children. . . . Who are you?"

- Where did he get his ideas? He resisted the common perception that he must come up with his ideas by watching his own kids. His ideas came from within himself and perhaps from his general observation of human nature.

- He was bothered by the perception of many that *Peanuts*, like most cartoons, was addressed primarily to children. He used children to people his strip, but he felt that what he was mainly dealing with, even when the focus was on Snoopy, covered the whole range of human nature.

• By this time people were beginning to find great depth in the simple *Peanuts* strips. Robert Short would soon come out with his best-selling *Gospel According to Peanuts* and would make a kind of industry out of interpreting Schulz. Sparky was flattered by this and found in Short a real friend. But when Short would label *Peanuts* as the cartoon of neo-orthodoxy, Sparky would say, "What's that?" (Actually, he would know a lot about neo-orthodoxy, but he would not consciously make himself a voice for that theology.)

• Sparky knew that he was bothered by some fears and anxieties. When he communicated this through the strip he was indeed walking in the shadows of a neo-orthodox theology. But he also felt that he had an optimism and that the *Peanuts* gang did too. Why would Charlie Brown keep on trying to kick Lucy's football? Why would Charlie Brown keep on trying to win baseball games? But, in his view, Charlie Brown had to keep on missing the football and losing the games for there to be humor in the situation.

• Sparky felt that his humor was a way of trying to deal with his insecurities and losses. He saw that in most of the other good humor we discussed.

In and around Sebastopol we did various things with Sparky and Joyce in the evenings. We went bowling.

"The first thing I noticed when I walked in here was a first-aid kit. . . . That sort of shook me up!"

Joyce was a licensed bowling instructor and tried to help us improve our game. Arlene and I had bowled less than a dozen times in our lives up to that point. Being nervous about the whole thing anyhow, my resulting score was something like a basement-hugging eighty. On the other hand Sparky had one of his best games ever, coming in just under three hundred. Another time we drove over to Santa Rosa to dinner. This would be his future home. The proprietor sent out word that our dinners would be compliments of the house. No wonder he would move to Santa Rosa, build No. 1 Snoopy Place, and contribute an indoor ice rink to the community.

Another time we drove down to San Francisco and ate in China Town. On that trip we went to the offices of Determined Productions and met Connie Boucher, the publisher of this small outfit who had brought out Sparky's first book, *Happiness Is a Warm Puppy*. It became a best-seller and helped to set the pace for the quality work that would come to be associated with the whole *Peanuts* enterprise.

In a few days, I had completed a rough draft of the text for the little book, and Sparky had pencil sketches of all the cartoons that would appear in it. We had faced up to most of the world's problems even if we had not solved them. In a few months the book came out and had a highly successful sale, far beyond what might be expected of a book about church-related education for preschool children. A mass paperback producer later brought out an edition that had a fabulous sale. As book editor I agreed with Sparky that on the hard-cover edition he would get a five percent royalty that was turned over to the Church of God Youth Fellowship. And I took one percent, the basis for my fortune today.

After doing the youth cartoons for several years, Sparky decided that he should take himself out of that series. He felt that he was growing too far from church youth. And he was under heavy pressure with the multiple development of the whole *Peanuts* enterprise with all the licensing arrangements. He continued to feel that he needed to keep close rein on all of that from a quality standpoint. He continued to create and draw the daily cartoon entirely by himself. We continued to keep in touch but in a much more limited way than when he was drawing a cartoon every other week.

"I can never get it through my head. . . . Was Jesus a grown man or was he a little baby?"

In 1963, Anderson College conferred an honorary doctor's degree on Sparky, and with the Sterners and other Anderson friends we hosted the Schulzes in Anderson. Their visit was cut short when word came that their son Craig had been hurt in a horseback riding accident. Sparky never was much a lover of travel and they had driven back by car from California. They immediately left for home with much anguish.

Along about 1979, Anderson College built a new fine arts center, with Sparky contributing major funding for the arts wing of that center. He requested that the name of that unit should honor his former pastor, Marvin Forbes. While in Anderson on that trip he joked that he had offered the college money for another building if they would name it after me and call it Hall Hall, something they seemed unwilling to do.

In the 1980s our son Doug began developing what he hoped would be a career in cartooning. He had been much influenced by Sparky through our family friendship. He sold cartoons to a range of national magazines and particularly the religious press. Finally, after a long developmental struggle he syndicated a daily and Sunday cartoon *Simple Beasts* through the Tribune Media Syndicate. It was introduced at a reception in a downtown Washington hotel at the same time as a new column by Pat Buchanan was being introduced by the syndicate. The strip got off to a good start and was appearing in major papers in Dallas, Los Angeles, San Francisco, Seattle, Baltimore, Orlando, and others. It even appeared in the Santa Rosa paper, Sparky's hometown. Sparky was a major supporter of the new strip, and was particularly influential in it appearing on the West Coast. But home difficulties were draining away Doug's creative energy. The strip reached a peak of about a hundred newspapers, not really enough to support the full-time work required to produce it. We all, including Sparky, were saddened to see it go.

My contacts with Sparky during the last decade or so of his life were limited largely to occasional phone calls about business matters left over from the earlier publications, to notes on special occasions like my retirement, and to Christmastime exchanges. His reduced contacts with the Church of God were a part of this. There were limited opportunities for such contacts to take place in and around Santa Rosa. He may also have been turned off from the Church of God because of the narrowness he was feeling in some of the people who did reach him and others seeking special favors because of the Church of God connection. He may also have felt that the failure of his marriage to Joyce raised something of a

barrier with the church. And the interests of his delightful new wife Jeannie may have taken him in other directions.

As the calendar turned toward the new century, there was considerable discussion about who might not be just the Man of the Year but the Man of the Century. A president like Franklin D. Roosevelt? A general like Dwight D. Eisenhower? A scientist like Albert Einstein? A humanitarian like Mother Theresa? Well, any such choice would not satisfy everyone and would be colored by one's personal philosophy and orientation. But there was considerable talk that such a person might well be Charles M. Schulz. And nobody would be more surprised or even aghast at such talk than Sparky himself. But few communicators grasped the spirit of the twentieth century person better than he did in his little family of *Peanuts* characters.

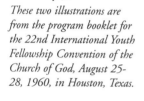

These two illustrations are from the program booklet for the 22nd International Youth Fellowship Convention of the Church of God, August 25-28, 1960, in Houston, Texas.

Few persons provided an art and a literature and a social commentary reaching more widely and consistently into human hearts than did the quietly perceptive Charles M. Schulz. Who reached around the world and into homes, schools, businesses, and churches more pervasively? Man of the century? Why not?

Acknowledgments

Charles Schulz cartoons © Warner Press, Inc. Anderson, Indiana All rights reserved Used by permission.

Peanuts: © United Feature Syndicate, Inc. Used by permission

I would like to thank my wife Avis for her suggestions and help in the creation of this book. Tammy Burrell helped in the technical portion of the book. The expertise of David Coolidge was invaluable in proofreading the copy. Karen Rhodes at Warner Press encouraged me to finish this project that I began over six years ago. My thanks to Arthur Kelly and Christie Smith Stephens for critiquing the work in progress.

Many thanks to all who contributed their memories of Sparky as well as personal correspondence. My sincere thanks also to Jeannie Schulz for her help and encouragement and to Charles Monroe Schulz for his influence on my life. For forty years Sparky's art and philosophy helped to shaped my life and I am grateful for his insights.

Jeannie and Sparky